WILD FLOWERS

of Britain & *Month by Month*

Wych Elm

I know a bank where the wild thyme blows,
Where oxlips and the nodding violet grows,
Quite over-canopied with luscious woodbine,
With sweet musk-roses and with eglantine.

William Shakespeare
A Midsummer Night's Dream
Act 2, Scene 1

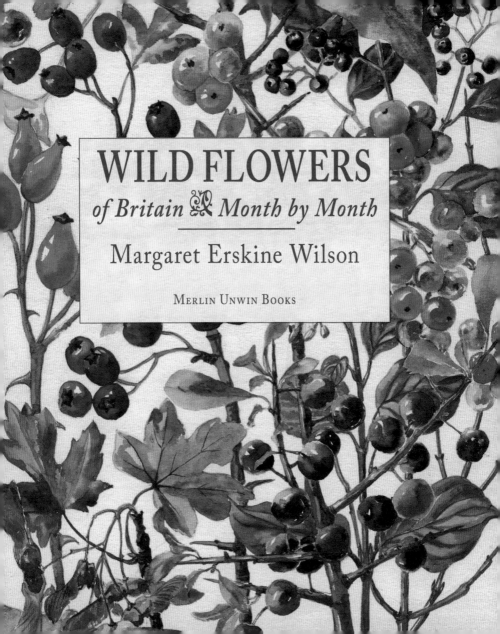

WILD FLOWERS

of Britain & *Month by Month*

Margaret Erskine Wilson

MERLIN UNWIN BOOKS

First published in Great Britain by Merlin Unwin Books, 2016.
Reprinted 2017, 2019, 2020, 2021

Copyright © Kendal Natural History Society 2016

Merlin Unwin Books
Palmers House, 7 Corve Street, Ludlow
Shropshire SY8 1DB   U.K.

www.merlinunwin.co.uk

The copyright holders assert their moral right to be identified with this work.
Edited by Judith Robinson
Designed and set in Minion by Merlin Unwin
Printed and bound by IMAK
ISBN 978-1-910723-31-9

Contents

Margaret Erskine Wilson, late President of Kendal Natural History Society, was a keen amateur botanist and water-colourist. In 1999, she donated to the Society 150 sheets of water-colour paintings representing British and Irish plants in flower and in fruit, painted *in situ* over many years and in various places.

At the time she gave the paintings to Kendal Natural History Society, she wrote:

Begun in 1943 for a friend who said, 'I might learn the names of flowers if you drew them for me, in the months they're in flower'!

After her death, I 'repossessed' them and continued the project until about 1990. I think about three-quarters of the British Flora are represented.

– Margaret Erskine Wilson
June 1999

Margaret Erskine Wilson
1915–2009

My Aunt, Margaret Wilson, was born in January 1915, the eldest child of the Reverend Tom Wilson, who was headmaster of Ardingly School, and her Mother was Ella Wilson, a talented violinist. She had two younger brothers: my late father, Hugh, and Andrew who emigrated to the USA soon after the end of the second world war. She was very close to her maternal grandfather, Henry Gibb, who was a notable painter and naturalist. It was from him that she learnt her own wonderful skill in painting.

Margaret was awarded a scholarship to Girton College Cambridge to study Modern Languages and completed her course in 1937. At that time women could study for degrees but were not allowed to be awarded the degree. It was with great pride that she and others returned to Cambridge some 40 years later to be awarded their degrees. After her time at Cambridge, she studied Textile Design at the Central School of Arts and Crafts, in London. She was studying there at the outbreak of the Second World War in 1939.

Margaret did not want to join a uniformed service for the war, so she became a teacher, intending to teach for the duration of the war. However, Margaret had found her vocation and remained a teacher.

She taught for some years at Bruton School for Girls in Somerset and then moved to Kendal in 1954 to teach modern languages at Kendal Girls High School, where I know she was greatly respected and admired by her pupils. Margaret finished her teaching career as Head of Modern Languages.

Soon after arriving in Kendal, Margaret became an enthusiastic member of the Kendal Natural History Society, leading field trips and acting for some years as secretary and later press correspondent. She became Vice-President of the Society in 2001 and President in 2007. She delighted in walking the fells; in her later years she would sit and look at them, remembering her walks. She exhibited her paintings at the Royal Horticultural Society's Botanical Art Show in London, and won silver medals on at least two occasions.

During the school summer holidays Margaret travelled widely and her paintings from that time include flowers from Afghanistan, Greece, Turkey, Cyprus and Crete. She visited her brother in New York State, USA, and painted flowers she found there. She enjoyed summer walking in the Swiss, Italian and French Alps, and delighted in the alpine flowers. As well as her paintings of flowers, she sketched and painted interesting buildings and architectural features, and some landscapes. Margaret remained interested in textile design, and recorded many costume details of medieval French and English design.

As 'Aunt Peggy' to my two sisters and me, she included regular visits to us as part of her travels. When we visited her in Kendal, she shared with us her passion for walking the fells and the local flora. She was always interesting to us, and interested herself in both ourselves and our families.

Margaret had a very full and energetic retirement including painting, walking and more amazing trips abroad. I am delighted that the paintings she donated to the Kendal Natural History Society are published here.

Felicity Guild

Editor's note

Margaret Wilson's paintings of flowers and fruit throughout the year, comprise over 1000 specimens and were compiled over a period of 45 years. Not only did the style of her paintings develop but the content of her pencilled notes on the back of each painting changed considerably. Names of the area or places where the specimens were painted are given on almost all the paintings, though in more detail on later ones. She also made cross references to the months of fruiting (where a flower is illustrated) and flowering (where the fruit is shown) throughout the project. Apart from this, the backs of early paintings give little information except occasional mention of interesting alternative English names.

This reflects Margaret's original purpose – to assist her friend in learning to recognise wild flowers – but after she had 'repossessed' the calendar (as she called the project) the notes became more detailed and often included the scientific names and notes on habitat. Individual paintings are not dated but clearly the small number of winter and autumn months were done in the early days whereas Margaret went on adding more pages for the spring and summer months and left some unfinished when ill health eventually brought an end to her painting. These unfinished sheets, extracts from which adorn the front and end pages of this book, show that the paintings were not planned as whole pictures but built up plant by plant, each painted *in situ*, and yet resulting in such pleasing compositions.

In preparing the collection of paintings into book form, I transcribed Margaret's notes, but also listed the English names as shown on the paintings, adding words in brackets where she gave only part of the full English name e.g. (Marsh) Arrow Grass. Where she used an unusual English name (sometimes a direct translation of the latin), I have added a footnote giving a more recognised name. I have also listed the scientific names, as far as possible, in their current form. The footnotes are mine.

I acknowledge the tremendous assistance given by Fiona Holman in checking the identities of the specimens illustrated and preparing the lists of scientific names.

Judith M. S. Robinson
Kendal Natural History Society
August 2016

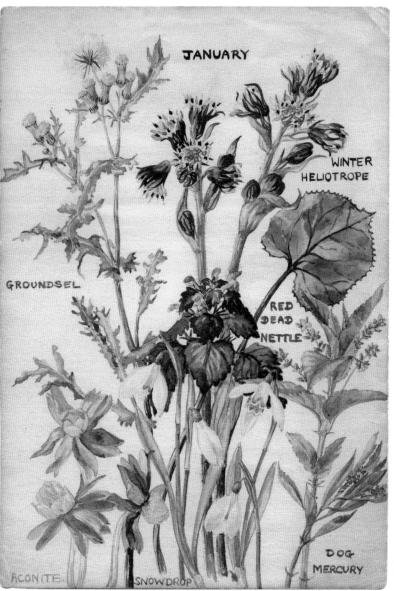

JANUARY

WINTER
HELIOTROPE

GROUNDSEL

RED
DEAD
NETTLE

DOG
MERCURY

ACONITE   SNOWDROP

Winter Heliotrope
Petasites fragrans

Groundsel
Senecio vulgaris

Red Dead-nettle
Lamium purpureum

Aconite
Eranthis hyemalis

Snowdrop
Galanthus nivalis

Dog Mercury
Mercurialis perennis

Margaret's notes:
West Walton

1

Hazel catkins
Corylus avellana

Green Daphne
Daphne laureola

(English) Elm
Ulmus procera

Alder catkins
Alnus glutinosa

Colt'sfoot
Tussilago farfara

Daisy
Bellis perennis

Lesser Celandine
Ranunculus ficaria

Bird's-eye
Veronica buxbaumii

False Strawberry
Potentilla sterilis

Margaret's notes:

Green daphne = Spurge laurel

Bird's Eye = Buxbaum's speedwell

False or Barren strawberry

Location: Bruton

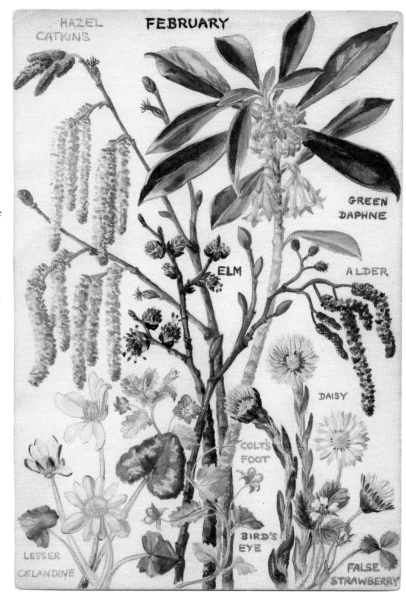

MARCH

GREEN HELLEBORE

(M)

(F)

ASPEN,
BLACK,
BALSAM,
AND
ITALIAN
POPLAR

WHITE
BUTTER
-BUR

BITTER-
CRESS

TRIQUETROUS
LEEK

VERNAL
WHITLOW GRASS

GOLDEN
SAXIFRAGE

YELLOW STAR
OF
BETHLEHEM

Green Hellebore
Helleborus viridis

Aspen
Populus tremuloides

Black Poplar
Populus nigra

Balsam Poplar
Populus balsamifera

Italian Poplar
Populus nigra italica

White Butterbur
Petasites albus

Bittercress*
Barbarea vulgaris

Triquetrous Leek
Allium triquetrum

Vernal Whitlow Grass
Draba verna

Golden Saxifrage
Chrysosplenium oppositifolia

Yellow Star of Bethlehem
Gagea lutea

Margaret's notes:

Location: mostly from Kendal, Cumbria; except Triquetrous Leek sent by C.R.A. from Penzance (also grows in Eire and Alderney)

*Bittercress also appears as Yellow Rocket on page 23

3

Butcher's Broom
Ruscus aculeatus

Gorse
Ulex europaeus

Lesser Periwinkle
Vinca minor

Primrose
Primula vulgaris

Wild Plum
Prunus institia

Pussy Palm (M)
Sallow/Willow (F)
Salix caprea

Sweet Violet
Viola odorata

Margaret's notes:

Gorse = whin
Wild Plum = bullace
Location: Bruton

4

MARCH

BUTCHER'S BROOM

PUSSY PALM (M)

GORSE

LESSER PERIWINKLE

PRIMROSE

WILD PLUM

SALLOW WILLOW (F)

SWEET VIOLET

MARCH

WHITE POPLAR

YEW

GOOSE-BERRY

BOX

DANDELION

White Poplar
Populus alba

Yew
Taxus baccata

(Wild) Gooseberry
Ribes uva-crispa

Box
Buxus sempervirens

Dandelion
Taraxacum officinale

Margaret's notes:

Yew fruit - Sept
Gooseberry fruit – June

Location: Bruton
(White Poplar from West Walton)

Sweet Gale or Bog Myrtle
Myrica gale

Stinking Hellebore or Setter-wort or Bear's-foot
Helleborus foetidus

Scurvy Grass
Cochlearia officinalis

Lungwort
Pulmonaria officinalis

Purple Saxifrage
Saxifraga oppositifolia

Crocus
Crocus vernus

Margaret's notes:

Locations: Westmorland & Furness; except Lungwort (New Forest), Purple Saxifrage (Ingleborough, also on Hellvellyn), Purple Crocus (Swarthmore), naturalised

Stinking Hellebore = Bear's Foot

Bog Myrtle - fruits August

Lungwort = Jerusalem Cowslip, Joseph & Mary, Lungwort: naturalised

6

Tea-leaved Willow
Salix phylicifolia

Black Currant
Ribes nigrum

Daphne
Daphne mezereum

Field Woodrush
Luzula campestris

Hairy Woodrush
Luzula pilosa

Crowberry
Empetrum nigrum

Romulea (Sand Crocus)
Romulea columnae

Ivy Speedwell
Veronica hederifolia

TEA-LEAVED WILLOW

BLACK CURRANT

DAPHNE

FIELD WOODRUSH

HAIRY WOOD RUSH

ROMULEA

IVY SPEEDWELL

CROW-BERRY

MARCH AND APRIL

Margaret's notes:

Daphne mezereum
Crowberry - Empetrum nigrum
Crowberry fruit - August
Daphne fruit - June / July
Black Currant fruit - July

Location: Westmorland; except Romulea (Dawlish Warren)

Mountain Currant*
Ribes alpinum

Crack Willow
Salix fragilis

White Dead-nettle
Lamium album

Wild Tulip
Tulipa sylvestris

Japanese Butter-bur
Petasites japonicus

Alternate-leaved Golden Saxifrage
Chrysosplenium alternifolium

Rock Hutchinsia
Hornungia petraea

Sheathing Cottongrass
Eriophorum vaginatum

Margaret's notes:

Crack Willow: like White Willow but not silky leaves; twigs break easily; by rivers.

Wild Tulip, rare

Japanese Butter-bur: in bud looks like a cauliflower! Naturalised on roadsides

Alternate-leaved Golden Saxifrage - rare form of opposite-leaved

Mountain Currant, uncommon, fruits Aug.

*Mountain Currant also appears on page 118 as Alpine Red Currant

8

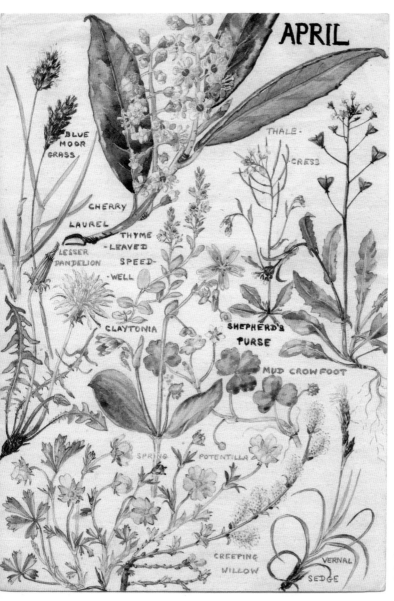

APRIL

Blue Moor Grass
Sesleria caerulea

Thale Cress
Arabidopsis thaliana

Cherry Laurel
Prunus laurocerasus

Thyme-leaved Speedwell
Veronica serpyllifolia

Lesser Dandelion
Taraxacum erythrospermum

Claytonia
Claytonia alsinoides

Shepherd's-purse
Capsella bursa-pastoris

Mud Crowfoot
Ranunculus tripartitus

Spring Potentilla
Potentilla tabernaemontani

Creeping Willow
Salix repens

Vernal Sedge
Carex praecox

Margaret's notes:

Kendal and Arnside (esp. Spring Potentilla & Lesser Dandelion)

Cherry Laurel - fruits October

9

White Willow (M & F)
Salix alba

Hornbeam
Carpinus betulus

Hybrid Oxlip
Primula vulgaris x P. veris

Greater Periwinkle
Vinca major

Butterbur
Petasites hybridus

Hairy Violet
Viola hirta

Margaret's notes:
Location: Bruton

APRIL

WILD CURRANT

KINGCUP

LARCH

WILD DAFFODIL

GOLDILOCKS

MOSCHATEL

WOOD VIOLET

FORGET ME NOT

Wild Currant
Ribes rubrum

Kingcup
Caltha palustris

Larch
Larix decidua

Wild Daffodil
Narcissus pseudonarcissus

Goldilocks
Ranunculus auricomus

Moschatel
Adoxa moschatellina

Wood Violet
Viola reichenbachiana

Forget Me Not
Myosotis arvensis

Margaret's notes:

Moschatel = Town Hall Clock

Kingcup = Mayblobs, Marsh Marigold

Daffodil = Lent Lily in Westmorland

Location: Sussex; except Moschatel from Bruton

(Pedunculate) Oak
Quercus robur

Pear
Pyrus communis

Drooping Sedge
Carex pendula

Wood Sorrel
Oxalis acetosella

Early Spider Orchis
Ophrys sphegodes

(English) Elm fruits
Ulmus procera

Mountain Speedwell *
Veronica montana

Margaret's notes:

Wood Sorrel = Alleluia in Czechoslovakia,

Bread & Cheese in Westmorland

Pear - fruits October

Oak - acorns in August (Durmast oak) & Sept.

Elm

flower - February

Location: Sussex & Bruton, except Spider orchis from Dorset, April/May

* usually called Wood Speedwell

APRIL

OAK

PEAR

DROOPING SEDGE

WOOD SORREL

EARLY SPIDER ORCHIS

ELM FRUITS

MOUNTAIN SPEEDWELL

APRIL

SUMMER SNOWFLAKE

CHERRY

OXLIP

ASH (M) (F)

COWSLIP

STITCH-WORT

MILKMAID

WOOD ANEMONE

WALL-FLOWER

DOG VIOLET

BLACK THORN

GROUND IVY

Summer Snowflake
Leucojum vernum

(True) Oxlip
Primula elatior

(Wild) Cherry
Prunus avium

Ash (M & F)
Fraxinus excelsior

Cowslip
Primula veris

(Greater) Stitchwort
Stellaria holostea

Milkmaid
Cardamine pratensis

Wood Anemone
Anemone nemorosa

Wallflower
Erysimum cheiri

Dog Violet
Viola canina

Blackthorn
Prunus spinosa

Ground Ivy
Glechoma hederacea

Margaret's notes:

Location: Glynde; except True Oxlip (Cambridge and Essex), only on boulder clay

Summer Snowflake = Loddon Lily (on the Loddon, wet woods in Berkshire)

13

(Silver) Birch
Betula pendula

Crab Apple
Malus sylvestris

Jack in the Hedge
Alliaria petiolata

(Common) Melick
Melica uniflora

(Common) Horse Tail
Equisetum arvense

Cornsalad
Valerianella locusta

(Field) Maple
Acer campestre

Tuberous Pea
Lathyrus tuberosus

Margaret's notes:

Jack in the Hedge = Garlic Mustard

Common Horsetail - Equisetum anvense

Crab Apple fruit - October

Location: Sussex

14

Horse Chestnut
Aesculus hippocastanum

Guelder Rose
Viburnum opulus

Whitebeam
Sorbus aria

Brooklime
Veronica beccabunga

Margaret's notes:

Horse Chestnut = House of Mary's Candles, fruits September

Guelder Rose, fruits September
Whitebeam, fruits September

Location: Bruton

Hairy Broom
Cytisus hirsutus

Meadow Saxifrage
Saxifraga granulata

Sheep's Bit
Jasione montana

Pale Heath Violet
Viola lactea

Sand Pansy*
Viola tricolor

Red Lady's Fingers**
Anthyllis vulneraria var. coccinea

Spathulate Fleawort
Tephroseris integrifolia

Margaret's notes:

Location: Anglesey except Hairy Broom and Sheep's Bit (St. David's)

*The Sand Pansy also appears on page 44 as the Wild Pansy and on page 68 as Heartsease.

Page 33 features two special varieties of this species.

**Red Lady's Fingers is a red form of the Common Kidney Vetch

16

MAY

HAIRY BROOM

MEADOW SAXIFRAGE

SHEEP'S BIT

PALE
← HEATH
VIOLET

SAND PANSY

RED LADY'S FINGERS

SPATHULATE FLEAWORT

ALKANET

HAIRY
VETCH

PENNY
CRESS

SALAD
BURNET

KNOTTED
CLOVER

WILD
CABBAGE

FIELD
FORGET
ME NOT

MAY

EARLY
GENTIAN

FENUGREEK

Alkanet
Anchusa officinalis

Hairy Vetch
Vicia villosa

Penny Cress*
Thlaspi arvense

Salad Burnet
Sanguisorba minor

Knotted Clover
Trifolium striatum

Wild Cabbage
Brassica oleracea

Field Forget-me-not
Myosotis arvensis

Fenugreek
Trigonella foenum-graecum

Early Gentian
Gentianella anglica

Margaret's notes:

Dorset (wild cabbage and early gentian) and Allerford, Minehead

* also appears as Stink-weed on page 116

17

Sycamore
Acer pseudoplatanus

Columbine
Aquilegia vulgaris

Great Horsetail
Equisetum telmateia

Toothwort
Lathraea squamaria

Yellow-and-Blue Forget-me-not
Myosotis discolor

Small Valerian (F & M)
Valeriana dioica

Marsh Violet
Viola palustris

Margaret's notes:

Location: Bruton, Columbine also Westmorland Great Horsetail also in New Forest

Sycamore fruit - September

18

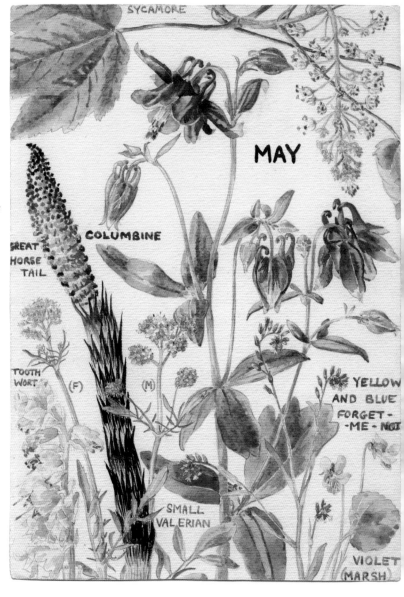

Red Campion
Silene dioica

Archangel
Limiastrum galeobdolon

Herb Paris
Paris quadrifolia

Bugle
Ajuga reptans

Water Avens
Geum rivale

Green-winged Orchis
Anacamptis morio

Silverweed
Argentina anserina

Germander Speedwell
Veronica chasmaedrys

May
Crataegus monogyna

Margaret's notes:

Archangel = Yellow Dead-nettle

May = Hawthorn (fruits in October)

Painted at Bruton, Somerset

Alder Buckthorn
Frangula alnus

Butter Dockin
Rumex obtusifolius

Chickweed
Stellaria media

Scots Pine
Pinus sylvestris

Teesdalia
Teesdalia nudicaulis

Spring Gentian
Gentiana verna

Pasque Flower
Pulsatilla vulgaris

Creeping Willowherb
Epilobuim brunnescens

Margaret's notes:

Creeping Willowherb: native of New Zealand, naturalised in Lake District

Alder Buckthorn fruit - August

Location: Westmorland except Pasque flower from Devil's Dyke, Newmarket, and Gentian from Upper Teesdale

20

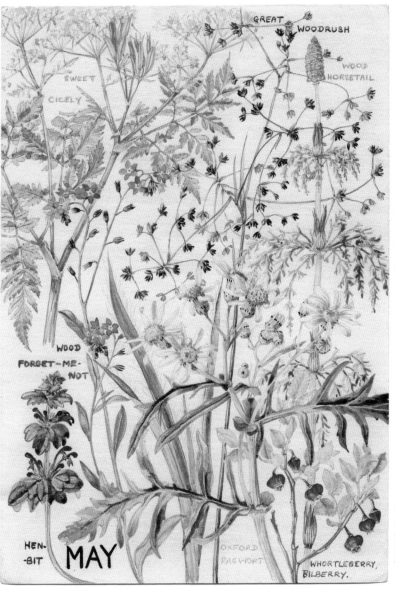

Great Woodrush
Luzula sylvatica

Sweet Cicely
Myrrhis odorata

Wood Horsetail
Equisetum sylvaticum

Wood Forget-me-not
Myosotis sylvatica

Hen-bit
Lamium amplexicaule

Oxford Ragwort
Senecio squalidus

Whortleberry, Bilberry
Vaccinium myrtillus

Margaret's notes:

Location: Kendal except Henbit from Calne; and Oxford Ragwort from Warwick

21

Mountain Cranesbill
Geranium pyrenaicum

Greater Celandine
Chelidonium majus

Dusky Cranesbill
Geranium phaeum

Jagged Cranesbill
Geranium dissectum

Herb Robert
Geranium robertianum

Dove'sfoot Cranesbill
Geranium molle

Long-stalked Cranesbill
Geranium columbinum

Margaret's notes:
Location: Bruton

22

MAY   MOUNTAIN CRANESBILL   GREATER CELANDINE

DUSKY CRANESBILL

JAGGED CRANES-BILL

HERB ROBERT

DOVE'S-FOOT CRANESBILL

LONG--STALKED CRANES--BILL

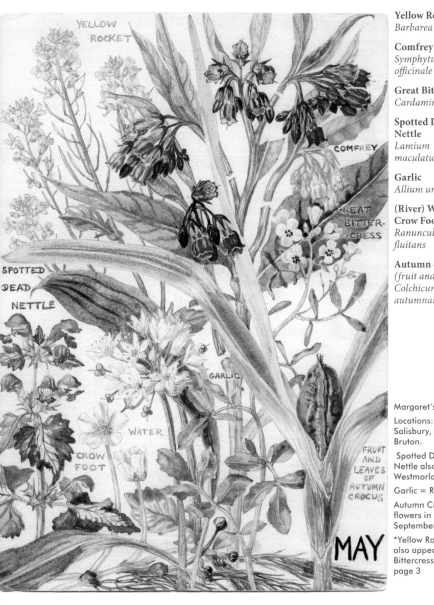

Yellow Rocket*
Barbarea vulgaris

Comfrey
Symphytum officinale

Great Bittercress
Cardamine amara

Spotted Dead Nettle
Lamium maculatum

Garlic
Allium ursinum

(River) Water Crow Foot
Ranunculus fluitans

Autumn crocus
(fruit and leaves)
Colchicum autumnale

Margaret's notes:

Locations: Salisbury, Oxford & Bruton.

Spotted Dead Nettle also Westmorland

Garlic = Ransoms

Autumn Crocus flowers in September

*Yellow Rocket also appears as Bittercress on page 3

23

Early Purple Orchis
Orchis mascula

Wood Spurge
Euphorbia amygdaloides

Bluebell
Hyacinthoides non-scripta

Fritillary
Fritillaria meleagris

Beech
Fagus sylvatica

Wild Arum
Arum maculatum

Bulbous Buttercup
Ranunculus bulbosus

Broom
Cytisus scoparius

Margaret's notes:

Fritillary = Snakeshead (more often April)

Wild Arum = Cuckoo-pint, Jack in the Pulpit, Lords & Ladies, Wake Robin

Beech Mast - October

Broom pods - October

Location: West Walton; except Fritillary from Oxford

24

PURPLE BROOMRAPE

ROUGH STAR THISTLE

MAY

SPANISH BLUEBELL

NARROW HARE'S EAR JERSEY ORCHID

DWARF PANSY.

SEA STOCK

STRIATED CATCH-FLY

BASTARD TOADFLAX

Purple Broomrape
Orobanche purpurea

Rough Star Thistle
Centaurea aspera

Narrow Hare's Ear
Bupleurum baldense

Dwarf Pansy
Viola kitaibeliana

Jersey Orchid
Orchis laxiflora

Sea Stock
Matthiola sinuata

Striated Catch-fly
Silene conica

Bastard Toadflax
Thesium humifusum

Spanish Bluebell
Hyacinthoides hispanica

Margaret's notes:

Channel Isles Flora

Jersey (sand-dunes of St. Quen's Bay and marshy reserve) and Alderney

Jersey Orchid - Orchis laxiflora (only Jersey & Guernsey in UK)

Spanish Bluebell (naturalised)

Sheep's Bit
Scabious*
Jasione montana

(no English
name)
*Senecio
spathulifolius*

Subterranean
Clover (fruit)
*Trifolium
subterraneum*

ANGLESEY
MAY
23 - 30
1985

Margaret's notes:

Location: Anglesey

May - June 1985
(Holyhead - South
Stack)

*sometimes called
simply Sheep's Bit,
as on pages 16
and 89

BETTYHILL

MAY 1984

OXYTROPIS
HALLERI

Margaret's notes:

Location: Farr Point
cliffs & Bettyhill
(Sutherland)

27

Perfoliate Claytonia or Miner's lettuce
Claytonia perfoliata

Columbine
Aquilegia vulgaris

Pyramidal Bugle
Ajuga pyramidalis

Creeping Speedwell
Veronica filiformis

Panicled Sedge
Carex paniculata

Three-Nerved Sandwort
Moehringia trinervia

Thyme-Leaved Sandwort
Arenaria serpyllifolia

Common Cotton Grass
Eriophorum angustifolium

Alpine Bear-berry
Arctostaphylos alpina

Lady's Slipper Orchis
Cypripedium calceolus

Margaret's notes:

Lady's Slipper Orchis: very hush-hush (Yorkshire)

[Drawn from a plant at least 80 years old, lifted from Ingleboro' then transported from Holehird, Windermere, to a garden in Kendal, where it flourished exceedingly]

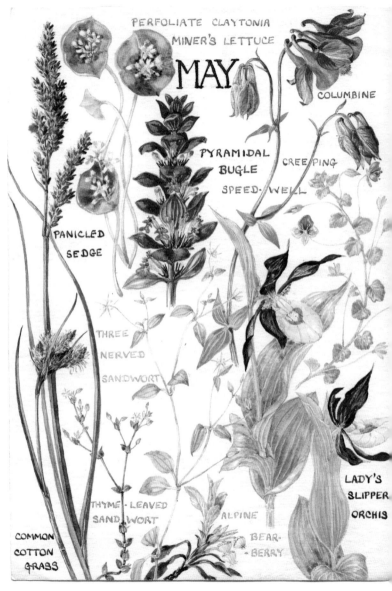

PERFOLIATE CLAYTONIA
MINER'S LETTUCE
MAY
COLUMBINE
PYRAMIDAL BUGLE
CREEPING SPEED-WELL
PANICLED SEDGE
THREE NERVED SANDWORT
LADY'S SLIPPER ORCHIS
THYME - LEAVED SAND-WORT
ALPINE BEAR-BERRY
COMMON COTTON GRASS

MAY

SOLDIER PLANTAIN

SOLOMON'S SEAL

COMMON VETCH

BUSH VETCH

HOLLY

NARROW-LEAVED VETCH

CREEPING BUTTERCUP

CROSSWORT BEDSTRAW

SHINING CRANESBILL

Soldier Plantain
Plantago lanceolata

Solomon's Seal
Polygonatum multiflorum

Common Vetch
Vicia sativa

Bush Vetch
Vicia sepium

Holly
Ilex aquifolium

Narrow-leaved Vetch
Vicia sativa ssp. nigra

Creeping Buttercup
Ranunculus repens

Crosswort Bedstraw
Cruciata laevipes

Shining Cranesbill
Geranium lucidum

Margaret's notes:

The narrow-leaved variety of Common (Single) Vetch, not Spring Vetch

Holly berries - December

Location: Bruton

Blinks
Montia Fontana

Meadow Saxifrage
Saxifraga granulata

Carnation Sedge
Carex panicea

Common Gromwell
Lithospermum officinale

Wood Stitch Wort
Stellaria nemorum

Spring Sandwort
Minuartia verna

Lily of the Valley
Convallaria majalis

Parsley Fern
Cryptogramma crispa

Mealy Primrose
Primula farinosa

Margaret's notes:

Location: Kendal (Cumbria)

Mealy Primrose = Bird's Eye Primula (Sunbiggin Tarn)

Blinks = Mossy Water Chickweed

Lily of the Valley (Arnside)

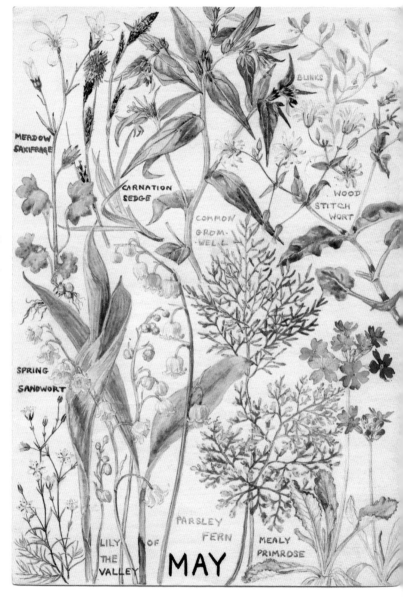

BLINKS

MEADOW SAXIFRAGE

CARNATION SEDGE

COMMON GROM-WELL

WOOD STITCH WORT

SPRING SANDWORT

PARSLEY FERN

LILY OF THE VALLEY

MAY

MEALY PRIMROSE

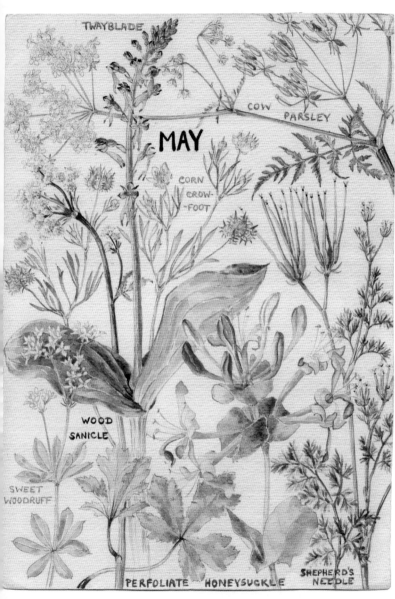

TWAYBLADE

COW PARSLEY

MAY

CORN
CROW-
FOOT

WOOD
SANICLE

SWEET
WOODRUFF

PERFOLIATE HONEYSUCKLE

SHEPHERD'S
NEEDLE

Twayblade
Listera ovata

Cow Parsley
Anthriscus sylvestris

Corn Crow-foot
Ranunculus arvensis

Wood Sanicle
Sanicula europaea

Sweet Woodruff
Galium odoratum

Perfoliate Honeysuckle
Lonicera caprifolium

Shepherd's Needle
Scandix pecten-veneris

Margaret's notes:

Cow Parsley = Queen Anne's Lace, Mother-die, Grandmother's blessing

Location: Bruton

English Stonecrop
Sedum anglicum

Lady's Fingers*
Anthyllis vulneraria

Pale Heath Violet
Viola lactea

Hairy Greenweed
Genista pilosa

ANGLESEY & ST. DAVID'S. MAY 1985

Margaret's notes:

Location: Anglesey & St. David's. May 1985

Pale Heath Violet (Cors Gogh Reserve, Anglesey)

Hairy Greenweed (St David's Head)

*more commonly known as Kidney Vetch

Common Milkwort
Polygala vulgaris

Common Milkwort (white-flowered form)
Polygala vulgaris ssp. collina

Meadow Saxifrage
Saxifraga granulata

Dog violet
Viola canina

Lady's Fingers (red form)*
Anthyllis vulneraria var. coccinea

Sand Pansies
*Viola tricolor ssp. curtisii
and Viola tricolor ssp. tricolor (var. Lepida)*

Margaret's notes:

Location: Anglesey

*Red Lady's Fingers is a red form of the Common Kidney Vetch

ANGLESEY
MAY 1985

33

Rowan
Sorbus aucuparia

Mealy Guelder Rose
Viburnum lantana

Blue Gromwell
Lithospermum urpurocaeruleum

Small-Flowered Buttercup
Ranunculus parviflorus

White Rockrose
Helianthemum appeninum

Buck's-Horn Plantain
Plantago coronopus

Bird Cherry
Prunus padus

Margaret's notes:

(Blue Gromwell and Small Buttercup from Bere Head,

White Rockrose from Brean Down)

Mealy Guelder Rose = Wayfaring Tree,

fruit - September

Birdcherry = Hickberry in Westmorland: smaller flowered in north. fruit - August

Mountain Ash = Rowan. fruit - August

Location: Bruton, Somerset

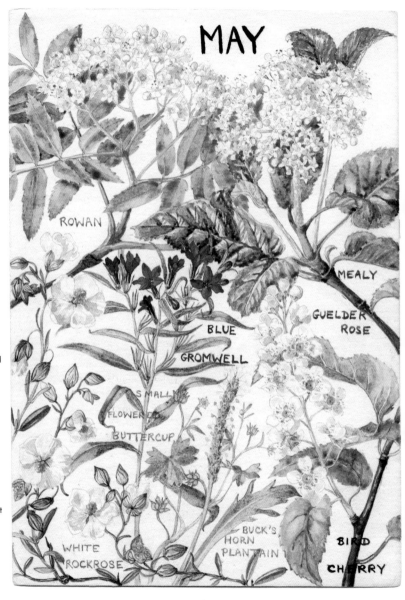

MAY

ROWAN

MEALY

GUELDER ROSE

BLUE

GROMWELL

SMALL

FLOWERED

BUTTERCUP

BUCK'S HORN PLANTAIN

WHITE ROCKROSE

BIRD CHERRY

BITHYNIAN VETCH MAY

JUNE

FLIX-WEED

STOCK

SHAMROCK

SPOTTED ROCK ROSE

HYBRID

AVENS

SMALL-FLOWERED CRANESBILL

SUBTERRANEAN CLOVER (FRUIT)

Bithynian Vetch
Vicia bythinica

Spotted Rockrose
Helianthemum guttatum

Flixweed
Sisymbrium sophia

Hybrid Avens
Geum rivale x urbanum

Stock
Matthiola incana

Small-flowered Cranesbill
Geranium pusillum

Shamrock
Oxalis sp.

Subterranean Clover (fruit)
Trifolium subterraneum

Margaret's notes:

Bithynian Vetch (Alderney), rare

Stock (Alderney, Cornwall), naturalised, sea cliffs

Spotted Rockrose (Alderney & Jersey)

Hybrid Avens: cross between Water Avens and Herb Bennet, occurs with both parents growing together

Small-flowered Cranesbill, not very common; dry places, walls

Shamrock - oxalis sp.: garden escapee (locally common e.g. in Alderney)

Marsh Arrow Grass
Triglochin palustris

Pyrenean Valerian
Valeriana pyrenaica

Parsley Piert
Alchemilla arvensis

(Black) Bog Rush
Schoenus nigricans

Bog Stitchwort
Stellaria uliginosa

Mossy Cyphel
Minuartia sedoides

Marsh Horsetail
Equisetum palustre

Dwarf Cornel
Cornus suecica

Whortle Willow
Salix myrsinites (F)

Cloudberry
Rubus chamaemorus

Trientalis
Trientalis europaea

Diapensia Lapponica
Diapensia Lapponica

Purple Milk-vetch
Astragalus danicus

Spring Squill
Scilla verna

Bear-berry
Arctostaphylos uva-ursi

Loiseleuria
Loiseleuria procumbens

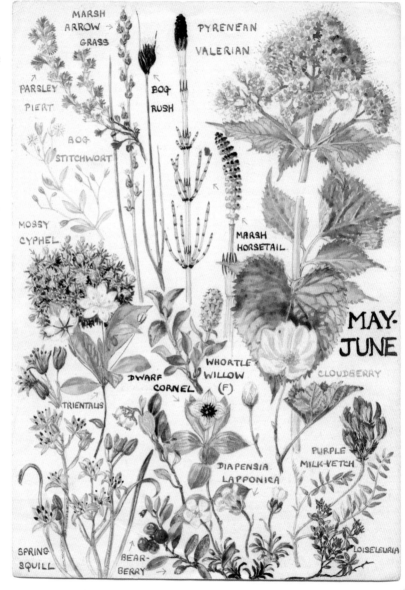

36

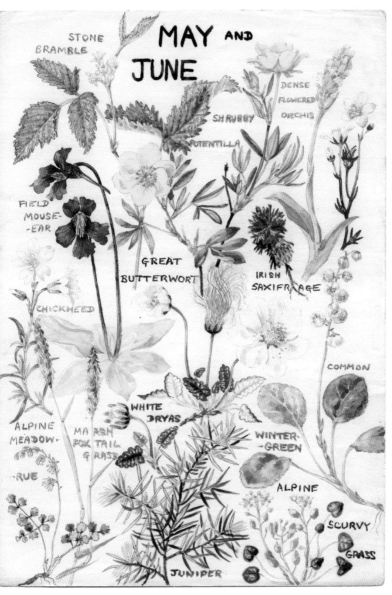

Stone Bramble
Rubus saxatilis

Dense-flowered Orchis
Neotinea maculata

Shrubby Potentilla
Dasiphora fruticosa

Field Mouse-ear Chickweed
Cerastium arvense

Great Butterwort
Pinguicula grandiflora

Irish Saxifrage
Saxifraga rosacea

Alpine Meadow-rue
Thalictrum alpinum

Marsh Foxtail Grass
Alopecurus geniculatus

White Dryas
Dryas octopetala

Common Wintergreen
Pyrola minor

Alpine Scurvy Grass
Cochlearia micacea

Juniper
Juniperis communis

Margaret's notes:

Location: Most from the Burren, Co. Clare

Common Wintergreen (Smardale Viaduct woods & Tebay [murdered by the M6])

Scottish Primrose
Primula scotica

Spring Squill
Scilla verna

Common Milkwort
Polygala vulgaris

Marsh Violet
Viola palustris

Spottted Orchid
Dactylorhiza sp.

N.W. SCOTLAND
May-June 1984

Margaret's notes:

N.W. Scotland May-June 1984

(Durness & Strathy Point & Bettyhill)

38

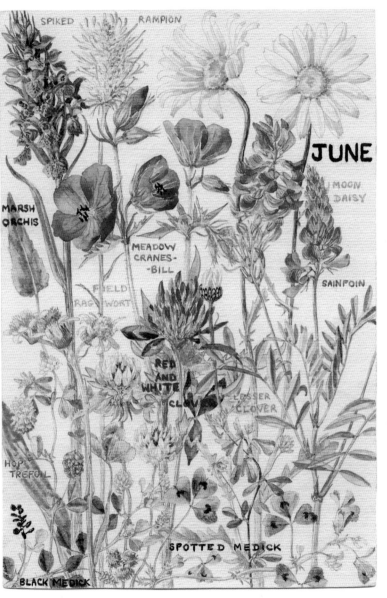

Spiked Rampion
Phyteuma spicatum

Moon Daisy
Leucanthemum vulgare

Marsh Orchis
Dactylorhiza sp.

Meadow Cranesbill
Geranium pratense

Field Ragwort
Senecio jacobaea

Sainfoin
Onobrychis viciifolia

Red Clover* and White Clover
Trifolium pratense and Trifolium repens

Lesser Clover
Trifolium dubium

Hop Trefoil
Trifolium campestre

Black Medick
Medicago lupulina

Spotted Medick
Medicago arabica

Margaret's notes:

Location: Bruton, except Spiked Rampion and Field Ragwort from Sussex

Moon Daisy = Horse-, Dog-, Ox-eye Daisy, Marguerite.

Sainfoin = Holy Hay

*Red Clover also appears on page 51, as Meadow Clover

Elder
Sambucus nigra

**Baneberry or
Herb Christopher**
Actaea spicata

**Tuberous
Comfrey**
*Symphytum
tuberosum*

Great Broomrape
*Orobanche
rapum-genistae*

**Alpine
Cinquefoil**
Potentilla crantzii

Margaret's notes:

Location: Kendal;
Baneberry and
Alpine Cinquefoil
(Ingleborough)

Elderberries -
October

40

Herb Bennet (Avens)
Geum urbanum

Dog Rose
Rosa canina

(Meadow) Clary*
Salvia pratensis

Cheddar Pink
Dianthus gratianopolitanus

Cut-leaved Saxifrage
Saxifraga hypnoides

(Common) Sorrel
Rumex acetosa

Buckbean
Menyanthes trifoliata

Wall Pepper Stonecrop
Sedum acre

Margaret's notes:

Sorrel =
Sour Dockin
(Westmorland)

Rose hips - October

Location: Cheddar

*Meadow Clary
also appears as
Meadow Sage on
page 59

41

Sea Couch Grass*
Agropyron junceiforme

Black Bryony
Tamus communis

Wild Strawberry
Fragaria vesca

Beech Fern
Phegopteris connectilis

Alpine Forget-me-not
Myosotis alpestris

Sand Sedge
Carex arenaria

Sand Cat's-tail Grass
Phleum arenarium

Coral-root
Corallorhiza trifida

Alpine Bartsia
Bartsia alpina

Creeping Willow
Salix repens

Margaret's notes:

Sea Couch Grass: dunes & slacks

Sand Cat's-tail Grass (Sandscale, Barrow-in-Furness)

Alpine Bartsia (Orton & Teesdale & Pennine limestone)

Alpine Forgetmenot (Little Fell)

Beech Fern (Kendal, Cumbria)

*Sea Couch-grass is also known as Sand Couch-grass.

It appears again on page 94 as Sea Quitch.

42

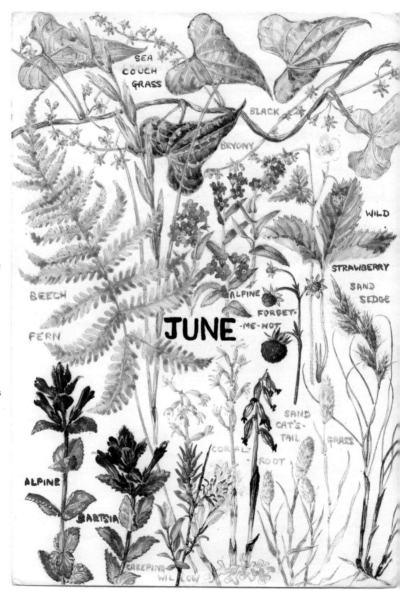

Narrow-leaved Vetch
Vicia angustifolia

Wallflower
Cheiranthus cheiri

Burnet Rose
Rosa spinosissima

Spring Squill
Scilla verna

LLANDUDNO &
ST. DAVID'S 1985

Margaret's notes:

Locations:
Llandudno & St.
David's; except
Spring Squill
(Anglesey &
Pembrokehire)

43

Globe Flower
Trollius europaeus

Wood Cranesbill
Geranium sylvaticum

Mountain Melick
Melica nutans

Hairy Rock-cress
Arabis hirsuta

Wild Pansy*
Viola tricolor

Yellow Pansy**
Viola lutea

Yellow saxifrage
Saxifraga aizoides

Sheathing Cotton-Grass
Eriophorum vaginatum

(Common) Cranberry
Oxycoccus palustris

Star Saxifrage
Saxifraga stellaris

Mountain Ever-lasting (F &M)
Antennaria dioica

(Common) Butterwort
Pinguicula vulgaris

Margaret's notes:

Location: Kendal & Lake District; except Yellow Pansy (Derbyshire & Teesdale)

*The Wild Pansy also appears on page 16 as the Sand Pansy and on page 68 as Heartsease.

**Yellow Pansy appears as Mountain Pansy on pages 95 and 104

GREAT
FEN
RAGWORT

JUNE

MARSH
PEA

SHADY
SAXIFRAGE

CREEPING
LESSER
SPEARWORT

Great Fen Ragwort
Senecio paludosus

Marsh Pea
Lathyrus palustris

Shady Saxifrage
Saxifraga umbrosa

Creeping Lesser Spearwort
Ranunculus flammula var. reptans

Margaret's notes:

Marsh Pea (Wicken Fen Reserve), Great Fen Ragwort (Cambridgeshire Fens), Creeping Lesser Spearwort (Ullswater), Shady Saxifrage (Weathercote Cave, Yorks)

45

Common Valerian
Valeriana officinalis

Spiked Star of Bethlehem
Ornithogalum pyrenaicum

Alexanders
Smyrnium olusatrum

Self-heal
Prunella vulgaris

Dwarf orchis
Orchis ustulata

Lesser Broomrape
Orobanche minor

Dyers Greenweed
Genista tinctoria

(Creeping) Cinquefoil
Potentilla reptans

Margaret's notes:

Location: Bruton; except Dwarf orchis from Yarnbury Camp, Alexanders from Wareham, Spiked Star of Bethlehem from Norton St. Philip

46

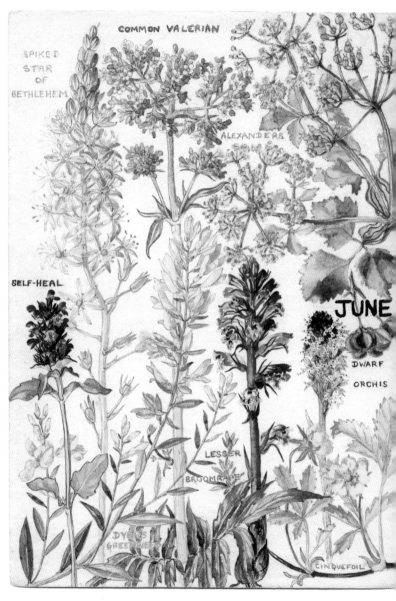

COMMON VALERIAN

SPIKED STAR OF BETHLEHEM

ALEXANDERS

SELF-HEAL

JUNE

DWARF ORCHIS

LESSER BROOMRAPE

DYERS GREENWEED

CINQUEFOIL

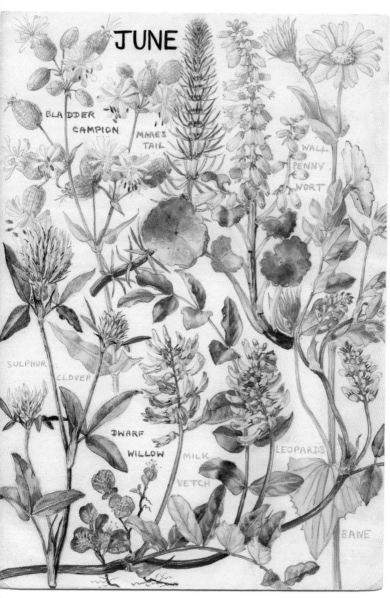

JUNE

Bladder Campion
Silene vulgaris

Mare's Tail
Hippuris vulgaris

Wall Pennywort
Umbilicus rupestris

Sulphur Clover
Trifolium ochroleucon

Dwarf Willow*
Salix herbacea

Milk Vetch
Astragalus glycyphyllos

Leopard's Bane
Arnica montana

Margaret's notes:

Location: Lake District and Kendal; except Sulphur Clover & Milk Vetch (Suffolk)

Dwarf Willow fruit - July

*Dwarf Willow also appears on page 104 as Least Willow

47

(Wild) Service Tree
Sorbus torminalis

Bay Willow
Salix pentandra

Charlock
Sinapis arvensis

Heath Bedstraw
Galium saxatile

Oak Fern
Gymnocarpium dryopteris

Field Rose
Rosa arvensis

Common Clubmoss
Lycopodium clavatum

Margaret's notes:

Location: Kendal & Lake District; except Service Tree (Sussex)

fruit - October

JUNE

SERVICE TREE

BAY WILLOW

CHARLOCK

HEATH BED STRAW

OAK FERN

FIELD ROSE

COMMON CLUB MOSS

JUNE

SMOOTH HORSE-TAIL

MARTAGON LILY

BALDMONEY, SPIGNEL, OR MEU

WILD GOOSE-BERRY

MARSH ANDROMEDA

LESSER BUTTERFLY ORCHIS

LESSER PROCUMBENT APIUM, MARSH WORT

HOARY ROCK-ROSE

FROG ORCHIS

Baldmoney, Spignel or Meu
Meum athamanticum

Smooth Horsetail
Equisetum laevigatum

Martagon Lily
Lilium martagon

Wild Gooseberry
Ribes uva-crispa

Marsh Andromeda
Andromeda polifolia

Lesser Butterfly Orchid*
Platanthera bifolia

Lesser Apium or Marshwort
Apium inundatum

Hoary Rock-rose
Helianthemum canum

Frog Orchis
Coeloglossum viride

Margaret's notes:

Location: Kendal; except Frog Orchid (also Wilts & Sussex)

Hoary rockrose (Scout Scar)

Gooseberry flower - March

49

Round-leaved Mint
Mentha suaveolens

Wild Celery
Apium graveolens

Common Mallow
Malva sylvestris

Oriental Mustard
Brassica juncea

Intermediate Sundew
Drosera intermedia

White Beaked Sedge
Rhynchospora alba

Black Spleenwort
Asplenium adiantum-nigrum

Alpine Clubmoss
Diphasiastrum alpinum

Margaret's notes:

Roundleaved Mint (Norfolk &Westmorland)

White Beaked Sedge: local; bogs

Intermediate Sundew (Beaulieu Heath, Wareham)

Celery: tidal riverbanks (Sussex); marshland (Kilynn)

Oriental Mustard (naturalised on the Bass Rock)

Alpine Clubmoss (Lake District fells)

Black Spleeenwort (Teesdale), limestone

ROUND- -LEAVED MINT

WILD CELERY

JUNE

COMMON MALLOW

ORIENTAL MUSTARD

INTERMEDIATE SUNDEW

WHITE BEAKED SEDGE

BLACK SPLEENWORT

ALPINE CLUBMOSS

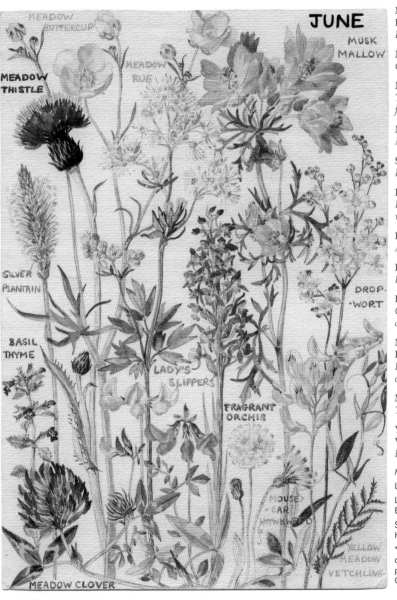

JUNE

Meadow Buttercup
Ranunculus acris

Meadow Thistle
Cirsium dissectum

Meadow Rue
Thalictrum flavum

Musk Mallow
Malva moschata

Silver Plantain
Plantago argenteu

Dropwort
Filipendula vulgaris

Basil Thyme
Acinos arvensis

Lady's Slippers
Lotus corniculatus

Fragrant Orchis
Gymnadenia conopsea

Mouse-ear Hawkweed
Pilosella officinarum

Meadow Clover*
Trifolium pratense

Yellow Meadow Vetchling
Lathyrus pratensis

Margaret's notes:

Location: Wareham

Lady's Slippers = Bird'sfoot Trefoil

Silver Plantain = Hoary Plantain

*Meadow Clover also appears on page 39, as Red Clover

51

Milk Thistle
Silybum marianum

Climbing Corydalis
Ceratocapnos claviculata

(Common) Cotton-grass
Eriophorum angustifolium

Pale Flax
Linum bienne

Storksbill
Erodium cicutarium

Slender Lotus
Lotus angustissimus

Bird's Foot
Ornithopus perpusillus

Red Rattle*
Pedicularis sylvatica

Evening Primrose
Oenothera biennis

Rough Clover
Trifolium scabrum

Burnet Rose
Rosa pimpinellifolia

English Stonecrop
Sedum anglicum

Sea Milkwort
Glaux maritima

Margaret's notes:
Location: Wareham

*more commonly called Lousewort

52

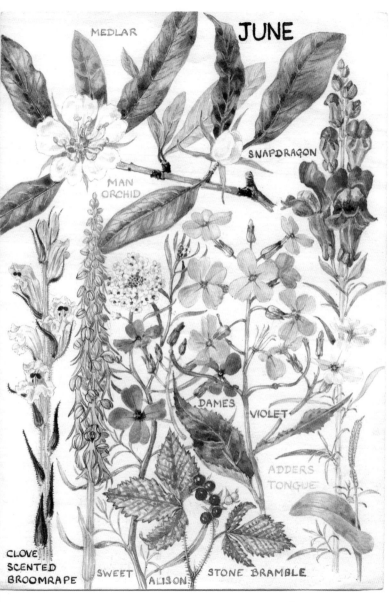

Medlar
Mespilus germanica

Snapdragon
Antirrhinum majus

Man Orchid*
Orchis anthropophorum

Dames Violet
Hesperis matronalis

Adder's Tongue
Ophioglossum vulgatum

Clove-scented Broomrape
Orobanche caryophyllacea

Sweet Alison
Alyssum maritimum

Stone Bramble (fruit)
Rubus saxatilis

Margaret's notes:

Medlar (saw it near Yeovil, in a hedge by a little church)

Clove-scented Broomrape (Sandwich golf-course), rare

Man Orchis (Queen Down Warren, Kent), rare

Sweet Alison (by sea, south of England & Channel Isles)

Snapdragon (old walls, castles etc. Lewes & Canterbury)

Adder's Tongue: in grass or under trees, rare

Hawkweed
Hieracium sp.

Jacob's Ladder
Polemonium caeruleum

Mountain St. John's Wort
Hypericum montanum

Lesser Stitch-wort
Stellaria graminea

Maidenhair Fern
Adiantum capillus-veneris

Spotted Cat's-ear
Hypochaeris maculata

Margaret's notes:

Location: Kendal

Mountain St. John's Wort (Grange over Sands)

Spotted Cats Ear (Humphrey Head), v. rare

Jacob's Ladder (Malham Cove)

Maidenhair (v. rare)

54

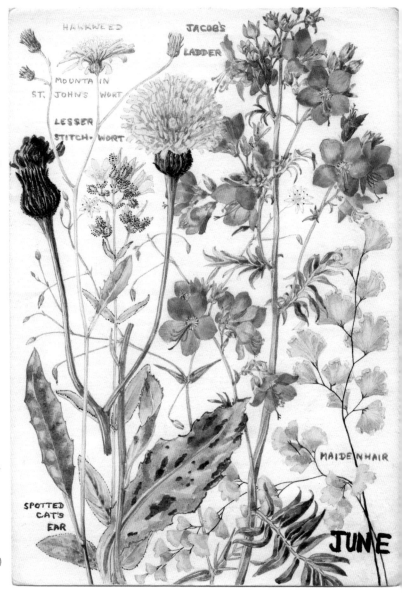

HAWKWEED

JACOB'S LADDER

MOUNTAIN ST. JOHN'S WORT

LESSER STITCH-WORT

SPOTTED CAT'S EAR

MAIDENHAIR

JUNE

JUNE

NOTTINGHAM
CATCHFLY

BARBERRY

LESSER
MEADOW
RUE

PORTLAND
SPURGE

MOTHER OF
THOUSANDS

Nottingham Catchfly
Silene nutans

Barberry
Berberis vulgaris

Lesser Meadow Rue
Thalictrum minus

Portland Spurge
Euphorbia portlandica

Mother of Thousands*
Cymbalaria muralis

Margaret's notes:

Location: Cheddar; except Nottingham Catchfly (from Bere)

Portland Spurge: also on sand dunes

Barberry = berberis

*more commonly known as Ivy-leaved Toadflax.

Tall Rocket
Sisymbrium altissimum

Marram Grass
Ammophila arenaria

Belle de Nuit
Oenothera biennis

Roseroot or Midsummer Men (M & F)
Rhodiola rosea

Alpine Sorrel
Oxyria digyna

Cow-berry
Vaccinium vitis-idaea

Marsh Pennywort
Hydrocotyle vulgaris

Margaret's notes:

Location: Lake District (Rose-root, Alpine Sorrel & Cowberry) and dune-slacks at Freshfield, Lancashire

Cowberry fruit - July

Belle de Nuit = Evening Primrose

White Stonecrop
Sedum album

Square-stemmed Willowherb
Epilobium tetragonum

Green Spleenwort
Asplenium viride

Hairy Stonecrop
Sedum villosum

Northern Marsh Orchis
Dactylorhiza purpurella

(Heath) Spotted Orchis
Dactylorhiza maculata ssp. ericetorum

Master-wort
Peucedanum ostruthium

Arenaria gothica (English Sandwort)
Arenaria norvegica ssp anglica

Alpine Kingcup
Caltha palustris ssp. minor

Alpine Penny-cress
Thlaspi caerulescens

Moon-wort
Botrychium lunaria

Margaret's notes:

Alpine Penny-cress (Littledale): likes lead-mine spoilheaps!

Master-wort (Dowthwaitehead, Ullswater): old pot-herb

Arenaria gothica (Ribblehead, Ingleton track)

57

Grass Vetchling
Lathyrus nissolia

White Bryony
Bryonia alba

Stinking Iris
Iris foetidissima

(Common) Spotted Orchis
Dactylorhiza fuchsii

Tamarisk
Tamarix anglica

(Greater) Butterfly Orchis
Platanthera chlorantha

Hound's Tongue
Cynoglossum officinale

Rue-leaved Saxifrage
Saxifraga tridactylites

Slender Thistle
Carduus tenuiflorus

Margaret's notes:

Somerset: Bruton & Polden Hills, except Grass Vetchling (Bolney, Sussex)

Spotted Orchis, *Orchis fuchsii*, is the variety found on basic soils

Stinking Iris fruit - September

White Bryony fruit - July

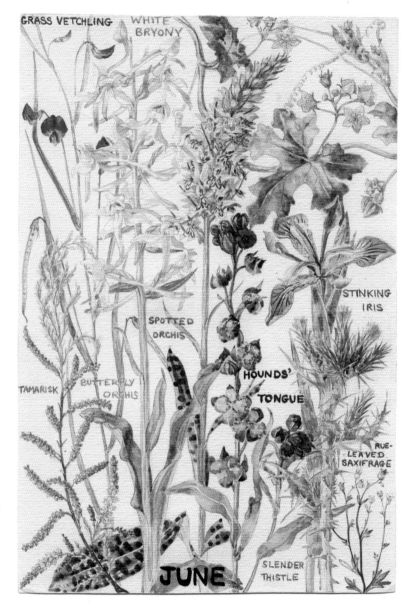

58

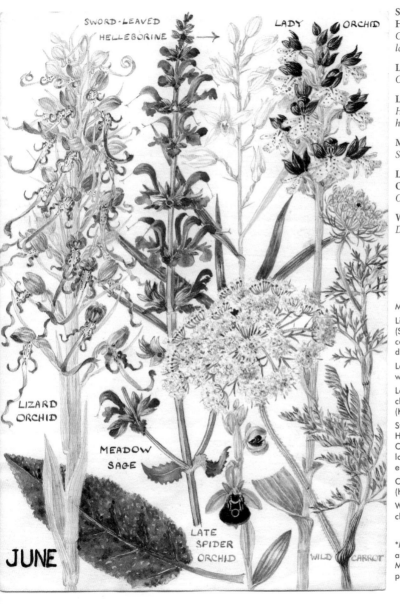

SWORD-LEAVED HELLEBORINE →

LADY ORCHID

LIZARD ORCHID

MEADOW SAGE

LATE SPIDER ORCHID

WILD CARROT

JUNE

Sword-leaved Helleborine
Cephalanthera longifolia

Lady Orchid
Orchis purpurea

Lizard Orchid
Himantoglossum hircinum

Meadow Sage*
Salvia pratensis

Late Spider Orchid
Ophrys fuciflora

Wild Carrot
Daucus carota

Margaret's notes:

Lizard Orchis (Sandwich golf course), chalk downs, rare

Lady Orchid: Chalk woods, rare (Kent)

Late Spider Orchid: chalk downs, rare (Kent)

Sword-leaved Helleborine - Cephalanthera longifolia / ensifolia:

Chalk woods, rare (Hants)

Wild Carrot: sea-cliffs (Kent)

*Meadow Sage also appears as Meadow Clary on page 41

59

Goutweed or Ground Elder
Aegopodium podagraria

Pignut
Conopodium majus

Wild Raspberry
Rubus idaeus

Hairy Hawkbit
Leontodon hispidus

JUNE

GOUTWED
or
GROUND
ELDER

PIGNUT

WILD RASPBERRY

HAIRY
HAWKBIT

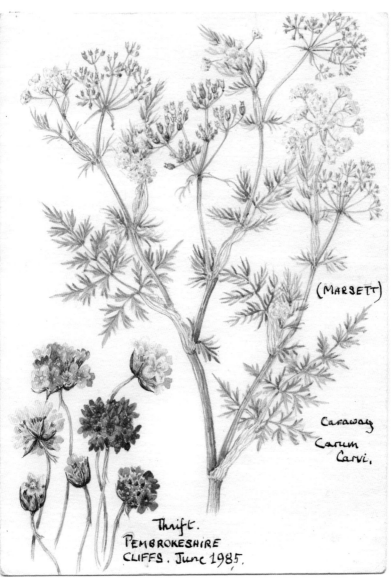

(MARSETT)

Caraway
Carum
Carvi.

Thrift.
PEMBROKESHIRE
CLIFFS. June 1985.

Margaret's notes:

Caraway - Carum carvi (Marsett)

Thrift = Seapinks - Armeria maritima

Location: Pembrokeshire cliffs, June 1985

Monkshood
Aconitum napellus

Bistort
Persicaria bistorta

Water Forget-me-not
Myosotis scorpioides

Ragged Robin
Lychnis flos-cuculi

Yellow Iris
Iris pseudacorus

Spindle
Euonymus europaeus

Corn Campanula
Legousia hybrida

Margaret's notes:

Location: Bruton; except Corn campanula from Cheltenham

Yellow Iris = Flag

Bistort = Easter Ledge

Spindle berries - November

JUNE

MONKSHOOD

BISTORT

WATER FORGET-ME-NOT

YELLOW IRIS

RAGGED ROBIN

SPINDLE

CORN CAMPANULA

Buckthorn
Rhamnus cathartica

Tea Tree*
Lycium barbarum

Hoary Cress
Lepidium draba

Yellow Rattle
Rhinanthus minor

Asparagus
Asparagus officinalis

Water Speedwell
Veronica anagallis-aquatica

Wall Speedwell
Veronica arvensis

Marsh Orchis
Dactylorhiza maculata (var. carnea)

Melancholy Thistle
Cirsium helenioides

Margaret's notes:

Locations: Kendal; except Buckthorn & Tea Tree from Bruton; Asparagus & Marsh Orchis (var. carnea) from Southport

*more commonly known as 'the Duke of Argyle's Tea-plant'

63

Corn Poppy
Papaver rhoeas

Wild Mignonette*
Reseda luteola

White Campion
Silene latifolia

Jack go to Bed at Noon
Tragopogon pratensis

Welsh Poppy
Meconopsis cambrica

Hawkbit
Leontodon sp

Margaret's notes:

Location: Salisbury; except Welsh Poppy from Allerford (also Westmorland)

Jack go to Bed at Noon = Goatsbeard

*Wild Mignonette also appears on page 117 as Dyer's Rocket.

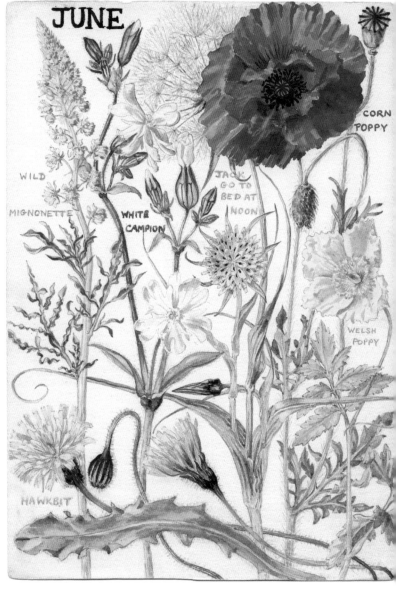

64

Horned Poppy
Glaucium flavum

Deadly Nightshade
Atropa belladonna

Fly Orchis
Ophrys insectifera

Henbane
Hyoscyamus niger

Bee Orchis
Ophrys apifera

White Helleborine
Cephalanthera damasonium

Horse-shoe Vetch
Hippocrepis comosa

Lady's Fingers*
Anthyllis vulneraria

Thrift
Armeria maritima

(Common) Milkwort
Polygala vulgaris

Musk Orchis
Herminium monorchis

Rockrose
Helianthemum nummularium

Margaret's notes:

Location: Lewes (chalk)

Thrift = Sea Pink

*more commonly known as Kidney Vetch

Cleavers, or Goosegrass, or Sweet-hearts
Galium aparine

Eye-bright
Euphrasia nemorosa

Foxglove
Digitalis purpurea

Sand Leek
Allium scorodoprasum

Marsh Water-cress
Rorippa palustris

Common Pink
Dianthus plumarius

Common Cow-wheat
Melampyrum pratense

Margaret's notes:

Location: Kendal & Fountains Abbey (Common Pink)

Common Cow-wheat drawn twice:

this Northern one has deeper yellow flowers than the Southern one

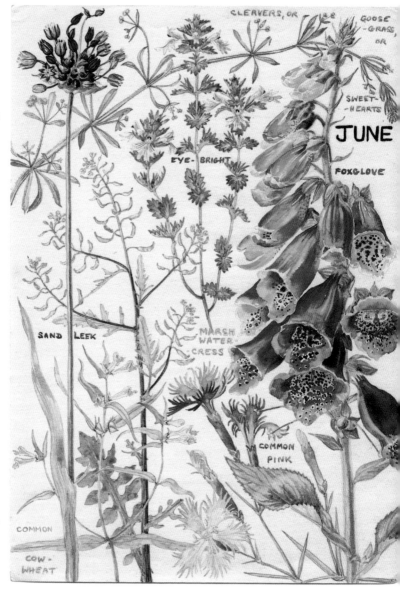

HONEYSUCKLE

SWEET
BRIAR

EEDLE
FURSE

HEDGE
BEDSTRAW

LADY'S
MANTLE

LOUSEWORT

COMMON
SPEEDWELL

JUNE

Honeysuckle
Lonicera periclymenum

Sweet Briar
Rosa rubiginosa

Needle Furse
Genista anglica

Hedge Bedstraw
Galium mollugo

Lady's Mantle
Alchemilla mollis

Lousewort
Pedicularis sylvatica

Common Speedwell
Veronica officinalis

Margaret's notes:

Honeysuckle - fruits August

Location: Salisbury

Creeping Yellow Water Cress
Rorippa sylvestris

Fox and Cubs
Pilosella aurantiaca

Lyme grass
Leymus arenarius

Horse Radish
Armoracia rusticana

Wall Whitlow Grass
Draba muralis

Heartsease*
Viola tricolor

Annual Knawel
Scleranthus annus

Margaret's notes:

Fox & Cubs: an introduced & rapidly spreading weed

Lyme Grass: sand dunes

Heartsease & Knawel: cornfields in S. & W.

*Heartsease also appears on page 16 as the Sand Pansy and on page 44 as the Wild Pansy.

Page 33 features two special varieties of this species.

CREEPING YELLOW WATER CRESS

JUNE

FOX AND CUBS

LYME GRASS

HORSE RADISH

WALL WHITLOW GRASS

HEARTSEASE

ANNUAL KNAWEL

JUNE

GREAT YELLOW WATERCRESS

WATER DROPWORT

CHERRY

MARSH STITCHWORT

ROUND-
-LEAVED
CRANES-
-BILL

BROOK-
-WEED

BIRDS
NEST
ORCHIS

BROAD
PONDWEED

Great Yellow Watercress
Rorippa amphibia

Water Dropwort
Oenanthe sp.

(Wild) Cherry
Prunus avium

Marsh Stitchwort
Stellaria palustris

Round-leaved Cranesbill
Geranium rotundifolium

Brook-weed
Samolus valerandi

Bird's Nest Orchis
Neottia nidus-avis

Broad Pondweed
Potamogeton natans

Margaret's notes:

Location: Bradford on Avon (except Bird's Nest Orchis from Wilton)

Cherry flowers - April

69

Cock's-Foot Grass
Dactylis glomerata

Tall Rocket
Sisymbrium altissimum

Wild Chamomile
Matricaria recutita

Field Cabbage
Brassica oleracea

COCK'S FOOT GRASS

TALL ROCKET

JUNE

WILD CHAMOMILE

FIELD CABBAGE

Margaret's notes:

Wild Chamomile: very like Scentless Mayweed (August) but scented

JUNE

CORN COCKLE

PLANTAIN THRIFT

PROLIFEROUS PINK

HOARY POTENTILLA

YELLOW VETCHLING

PURPLE VIPER'S BUGLOSS

SCOTTISH ASPHODEL

BASTARD BALM

ASARABACCA

BITTER MILKWORT

Corn Cockle
Agrostemma githago

Plantain Thrift
Armeria pseudarmeria

Proliferous Pink
Petrorhagia prolifera

Hoary Potentilla
Potentilla argentea

Yellow Vetchling
Lathyrus aphaca

Purple Viper's Bugloss
Echium plantagineum

Scottish asphodel
Tofieldia pusilla

Bastard Balm
Melittis melissophyllum

Asarabacca
Asarum europaeum

Bitter Milkwort
Polygala amara

Margaret's notes:

Plantain Thrift (Channel Islands)

Hoary Potentilla (Leziate golf course, Norfolk)

Proliferous Pink (Jersey)

Bastard Balm (Devonshire Lanes)

Asarabacca (Lingen, Welsh border)

Scottish Asphodel (Teesdale & Scotland)

Small White Orchid
Leucorchis albida

Stiff Sedge
Carex bigelowii

Three-leaved Rush
Juncus trifidus

Peppermint
Mentha piperita

Lyme Grass
Elymus arenarius

Tree Lupin
Lupinus arboreus

Spiked Woodrush
Luzula spicata

Horse Mint
Mentha longifolia

Greater Dodder
Cuscuta europaea

Margaret's notes:

Horse Mint (Braithwaite)

Peppermint (Kentmere)

Small White Orchid (Skye)

Tree Lupin - Lupinus arboreus (Alderney, Walney Island): naturalised, railway banks

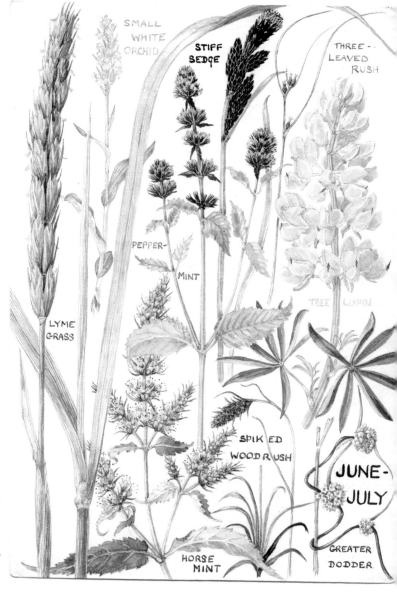

SMALL WHITE ORCHID

STIFF SEDGE

THREE-LEAVED RUSH

PEPPER-MINT

LYME GRASS

TREE LUPIN

SPIKED WOODRUSH

JUNE-JULY

GREATER DODDER

HORSE MINT

IRISH
SPURGE

JUNE
- JULY

REFLEX-
-LEAVED
STONECROP

ADDER'S
TONGUE

LILY
OF
THE
VALLEY

DAPHNE

CRIMSON
CLOVER

ISLE
OF MAN
CABBAGE

RED
BROOM-
RAPE

ANGULAR
SOLOMON'S-
SEAL

BLUE PIMPERNEL

Irish Spurge
Euphorbia hyberna

Reflex-leaved Stonecrop
Sedum reflexum

Adder's Tongue
Ophioglossum vulgatum

Lily of the Valley in fruit
Convallaria majalis

Crimson Clover
Trifolium incarnatum

Daphne in fruit
Daphne mezereum

Isle of Man Cabbage
Rhynchosinapis monensis

Red Broomrape
Orobanche rubra

Angular Solomon's Seal
Polygonatum odoratum

Blue Pimpernel
Anagallis foemina

Margaret's notes:

Irish Spurge (Cork & Kerry)

Reflex-leaved Stonecrop: on walls, naturalised (Devon).

Crimson Clover: once grown for fodder in the South; now uncommon

Isle of Man Cabbage (Cumbrian coast)

Angular Solomon's Seal: limestone in North, rare

Red Broomrape: (Lizard Head)

73

Portuguese Laurel
Prunus lusitanica

Water Figwort
Scrophularia auriculata

Hoary Willowherb
Epilobium parviflorum

Common St. John's Wort
Hypericum perforatum

Maiden Pink
Dianthus deltoides

Hedge Woundwort
Stachys sylvatica

Viviparous Bistort
Polygonum viviparum

Spiked Water Milfoil
Myriophyllum spicatum

Water Cress
Nasturtium officinale

Margaret's notes:

Common St. John's Wort: perforate

Maiden Pink (Nibthwaite, Coniston)

Viviparous Bistort (Helvellyn & Teesdale)

Spiked Water Milfoil (Westmorland & Holy Island)

JUNE–JULY

PORTUGUESE LAUREL

WATER FIGWORT

HOARY WILLOW HERB

COMMON ST. JOHN'S WORT

MAIDEN PINK

HEDGE WOUNDWORT

VIVI - PAROUS BISTORT

SPIKED WATER MILFOIL

WATER CRESS

JULY

SPREADING CAMPANULA

KEELED GARLIC

MOUSE-EAR CHICKWEED

CANADIAN WATER WEED

PERFOLIATE PONDWEED

CURLY PONDWEED

THORN APPLE

Spreading Campanula
Campanula patula

Keeled Garlic
Allium carinatum

Mouse-ear Chickweed
Cerastium fontanum

Canadian Water Weed
Elodea canadensis

Perfoliate Pondweed
Potamogeton perfoliatus

Curly Pondweed
Potamogeton crispus

Thorn Apple
Datura stramonium

Margaret's notes:

Spreading Campanula (Herefordshire), rare

Keeled Garlic: introduced, casual (Galgate, Lancaster)

Thorn Apple: very poisonous weed of cultivation, occurs occasionally in potato fields etc.

(This specimen drawn in Afghanistan where it is abundant)

Yellow Sorrel
Oxalis stricta

Alpine Catchfly
Lychnis alpina

Moss Campion
Silene acaulis

Field Gentian
Gentianella campestris

Lady's Bedstraw
Galium verum

Sea-shore Centaury
Centaurium littorale

Spanish Catchfly
Silene otites

Oyster plant
Mertensia maritima

Margaret's notes:

Spanish Catchfly (Holland & Norfolk)

Alpine Catchfly (Hobcarton Crag, Cumberland, its only English station)

Oyster Plant (Walney Island [now extinct] & Scotland)

Moss Campion (Helvellyn & Scotland)

Field Gentian (Mull & Wales)

Yellow Sorrel: when young - upright with green leaves; when mature - creeping with purple leaves; common as garden weeds.

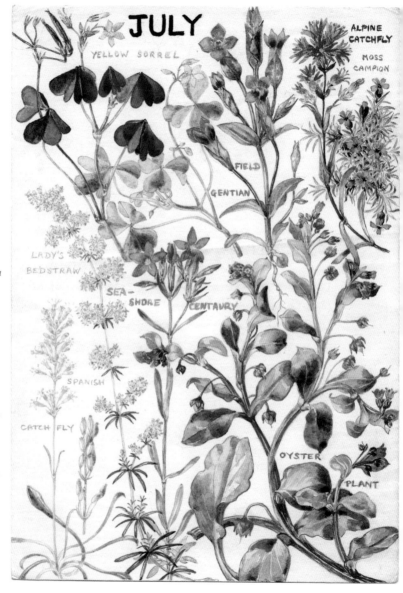

JULY

YELLOW SORREL

ALPINE CATCHFLY

MOSS CAMPION

FIELD GENTIAN

LADY'S BEDSTRAW

SEA-SHORE CENTAURY

SPANISH CATCH FLY

OYSTER PLANT

JULY

ROUGH-HEADED POPPY

TANSY

FEVERFEW

ORANGE
BALSAM

RED HEMP-
-NETTLE

MANY
SEEDED
GOOSEFOOT

Tansy
*Tanacetum
vulgare*

Feverfew
*Tanacetum
parthenium*

**Rough-headed
Poppy**
Papaver hybridum

Orange Balsam
*Impatiens
capensis*

Red Hemp-nettle
*Galeopsis
angustifolia*

**Many-seeded
Goosefoot**
*Chenopodium
polyspermum*

Margaret's notes:

Telscombe (except
Orange Balsam
from Wey valley)

Dark Mullein
Verbascum nigrum

Moth Mullein
Verbascum blattaria

Lucerne
Medicago falcata

Great Mullein
Verbascum thapsus

Clustered Clover
Trifolium glomeratum

Margaret's notes:

Location:
Telscombe & Bolney

Great Mullein =
Church Candle

Welted Thistle
Carduus crispus

Sharp Rush
Juncus acutus

Branched Bur-reed
Sparganium erectum

Smith's Cress*
Lepidum heterophyllum

Mimulus**
Mimulus guttatus

Wild Raspberry
Rubus idaeus

Pale Willowherb
Epilobium roseum

Margaret's notes:

Sharp Rush (Braunton Burrows)

Mimulus - the small-spotted form - Mimulus guttatus.

Smith's (or Downy) Cress - Lepidum Smithii or heterophyllum

Pale Willow Herb - Epilobium roseum

*usually known as Smith's Pepperwort

**this species also appears on page 89 with the English name Monkey Musk

Prickly Lettuce
Lactuca serriola

Larkspur
Consolida ajacis

Dittander (or Dittany)
Lepidium latifolium

False Water-cress
(Procumbent Apium)

Apium nodiflorum

PRICKLY
LETTUCE

LARKSPUR

JULY

DITTANDER

Margaret's notes:

Dittany (Dittander on plate): sandy soil near sea (Suffolk)

Larkspur: once a cornfield weed; naturalised in waste places

(Cambridge railway station)

FALSE
WATER-
CRESS
(PROCUMBENT
APIUM)

80

JULY

GREAT REED MACE

SLENDER VETCH

HOUSE LEEK

HAIRY ST. JOHN'S WORT

SPIKED SPEED -WELL

WHITE WATER LILY

Great Reed Mace
Typha latifolia

Slender Vetch
Vicia tetrasperma

House Leek
Sempervivum tectorum

Hairy St. John's Wort
Hypericum hirsutum

(Western) Spiked Speedwell
Veronica Spicata ssp. hybrida

White Water Lily
Nymphaea alba

Margaret's notes:

Location: Kendal and Sussex

Western Spiked Speedwell - Veronica Spicata ssp. hybrida (Humphrey Head)

Great Reed Mace: sometimes wrongly called Bulrush

(Narrow-leaved) Everlasting Pea
Lathyrus sylvestris

Teazel
Dipsacus fullonum

Pepper Saxifrage
Silaum silaus

Common Bladderwort*
Utricularia vulgaris

Small Fleabane
Pulicaria vulgaris

Spotted Persicaria
Persicaria maculosa

Margaret's notes:

Location: Bruton & Sedgemoor (Teazel, Bladderwort); Everlasting Pea (Cogley wood)

*this also appears on page 109 as Greater Bladderwort, its normal English name. "Common" is a translation of the scientific name.

EVERLASTING PEA

TEAZEL

JULY

PEPPER SAXIFRAGE

SMALL FLEA-BANE

COMMON

BLADDER WORT

SPOTTED

PERSICARIA

JULY

ROBIN'S PINCUSHION

NIPPLEWORT

FIELD SCABIOUS

WOODY NIGHTSHADE

VIPER'S BUGLOSS.

BOG ASPHODEL

SCARLET PIMPERNEL

FIELD MADDER

Robin's Pincushion
Dipoloepis rosae

Nipplewort
Lapsana communis

Field Scabious
Knautia arvensis

Woody Nightshade
Solanum dulcamara

Scarlet Pimpernel
Anagallis arvensis

Viper's Bugloss
Echium vulgare

Bog Asphodel
Narthecium ossifragum

Field Madder
Sherardia arvensis

Margaret's notes:

Location: West Walton; except Bog Asphodel from Ashdown Forest & Viper's Bugloss from Suffolk: chalk

83

Caraway
Carum carvi

Purple Salsify
Tragopogon porrifolius

Berberis
Berberis vulgaris

Flax
Linum usitatissimum

Greater Plantain
Plantago major

Bitter Candytuft
Iberis amara

Margaret's notes:

Salsify and Flax: occasional escapes from cultivation

Berberis (Mendips)

Candytuft (Chilterns), chalk

Caraway (Marsett, Wensleydale)

CARAWAY   PURPLE SALSIFY

BERBERIS

JULY

FLAX

GREATER PLANTAIN

BITTER CANDYTUFT

84

July 14ᵗʰ
1985
Fen ditch
near Soham.

Great Fen
Ragwort
Senecio paludosus

Hemlock Water Dropwort
Oenanthe crocata

Prickly Sow Thistle
Sonchus asper

Sheeps's Sorrel
Rumex acetosella

Small Fumitory
Fumaria officinalis

JULY

HEMLOCK WATER DROPWORT

PRICKLY SOW THISTLE

SHEEPS SORREL

SMALL FUMITORY

Margaret's notes:

Fumitory - Fumaria officinalis

86

BLUE SOWTHISTLE

WART CRESS

WATER RAGWORT

WOOD VETCH

LESSER TWAYBLADE

JULY

Blue Sowthistle
Cicerbita macrophylla

Wart Cress
Coronopus squamatus

Water Ragwort
Senecio hydrophilus

Wood Vetch
Vicia sylvatica

Lesser Twayblade
Listera cordata

Margaret's notes:

Blue Sowthistle: garden escape (we saw it at Thornton le Dale)

Lesser Twayblade (North & Scotland): rare; sphagnum bog or pine wood

Wood Vetch: uncommon (Langholm)

Purple-veined Geranium
Geranium versicolor

Tree Mallow
Lavatera arborea

Blood-red Cranesbill
Geranium sanguineum

Madder
Rubia peregrina

Sea Rocket
Cakile maritima

Autumnal Squill
Prospero autumnale

Great Burnet
Sanguisorba officinalis

Margaret's notes:

Location: Cornwall (Gweek & Lizard)

Bloody ('Blood-red' on plate) Cranesbill (Westmorland, Walney Is. etc.)

88

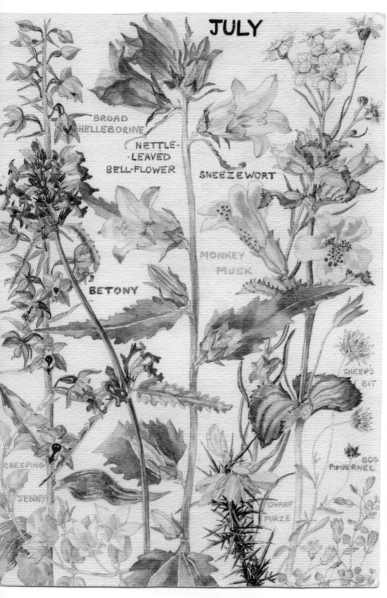

JULY

Broad Helleborine
Epipactis helleborine

Nettle-leaved Bellflower
Campanula trachelium

Sneezewort
Achillea ptarmica

Monkey Musk*
Mimulus guttatus

Betony
Stachys officinalis

Sheep's Bit
Jasione montana

Creeping Jenny
Lysimachia nummularia

Bog Pimpernel
Anagallis tenella

Dwarf Furze
Ulex gallii

Margaret's notes:

Location: Shropshire (between Ludlow & Church Stretton)

Creeping Jenny = Herb Twopence, Moneywort

*this also occurs on page 79 under the name 'Mimulus'

Cornflower
Centaurea cyanus

Greater Knapweed
Centaurea scabiosa

Spiny Restharrow
Ononis spinosa

Wood Sage
Teucrium scorodonia

Toad Flax
Linaria vulgaris

Felwort Gentian
Gentianella amarella

Sea Campion
Silene maritima

Star Thistle
Centaurea calcitrapa

Dwarf Thistle
Cirsium acaule

Margaret's notes:

Locations: Sussex, Cambridgeshire & Berkshire (cornflower)

CORNFLOWER

JULY

GREATER KNAP WEED

SPINY REST HARROW

WOOD SAGE

TOAD FLAX

FELWORT GENTIAN

SEA CAMPION

STAR THISTLE

DWARF THISTLE

SLENDER KNAPWEED

JULY

MILK PARSLEY

LEMON BALM

YELLOW BIRD'S NEST

LARGER WILD THYME

Slender Knapweed
Centaurea nigra ssp. nemoralis

Milk Parsley
Thyselium palustre

Larger Wild Thyme
Thymus pulegioides

Lemon Balm
Melissa officinalis

Yellow Bird's-nest
Monotropa hypopitys

Margaret's notes:

Larger Wild Thyme and Slender Knapweed (Wiltshire downs)

Milk Parsley (Strumpshaw Fen)

Lemon Balm (South Cadbury), naturalised

Yellow Bird's-nest (Sandscale Haws), duneslacks, saprophyte

Caper Spurge
Euphorbia lathyris

Dwarf Spurge
Euphorbia exigua

Northern
Bedstraw
Galium boreale

Canadian
Fleabane
*Conyza
canadensis*

Perennial Flax
Linum perenne

Grey (Field)
Speedwell
Veronica polita

Sickle Medick
*Medicago sativa
ssp. falcata*

Margaret's notes:

Caper Spurge:
naturalised in many
places

Northern Bedstraw
and Perrenial Flax
(Westmorland),
limestone

Sickle Medick
(Suffolk)

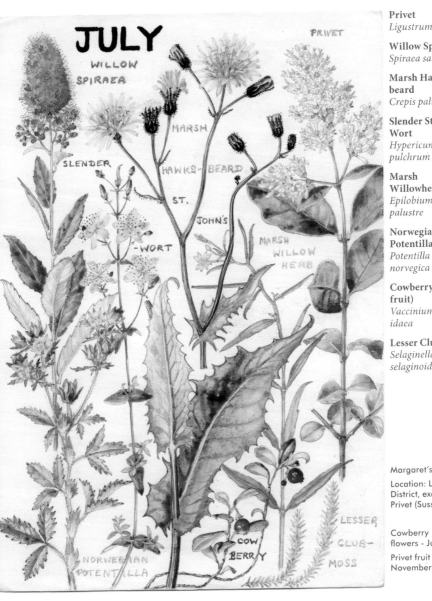

JULY

WILLOW SPIRAEA

PRIVET

SLENDER

MARSH

HAWKS-BEARD

ST.

JOHN'S

-WORT

MARSH WILLOW HERB

COW BERRY

NORWEGIAN POTENTILLA

LESSER CLUB-MOSS

Privet
Ligustrum vulgare

Willow Spiraea
Spiraea salicifolia

Marsh Hawks-beard
Crepis paludosa

Slender St John's Wort
Hypericum pulchrum

Marsh Willowherb
Epilobium palustre

Norwegian Potentilla
Potentilla norvegica

Cowberry (in fruit)
Vaccinium vitis-idaea

Lesser Clubmoss
Selaginella selaginoides

Margaret's notes:

Location: Lake District, except Privet (Sussex)

Cowberry flowers - June

Privet fruit - November

93

Marsh Thistle
Cirsium palustre

(Great) Fen Sedge
Cladium mariscus

Single Bur-reed
Sparganium emersum

Sea Quitch*
Agropyron junceiforme

Sea Chamomile
Matricaria maritima

Sea Plantain
Plantago maritima

Floating Bur-reed
Sparganium angustifolium

Blackcurrant (in fruit)
Ribes nigrum

Long Pondweed
Potamogeton praelongus

Margaret's notes:

Blackcurrant flowers - May/April

*more commonly known as Sand Couch-grass. But see also page 42 where it is called Sea Couch-grass.

94

JULY

MARSH THISTLE

FEN SEDGE

SINGLE BUR-REED

SEA QUITCH

SEA CHAMOMILE

SEA PLANTAIN

FLOATING BUR-REED

BLACK CURRANT

LONG PONDWEED

JULY

ALPINE
LETTUCE

BLACK
SEDGE

MUD
SEDGE

LADY'S
MANTLE

YELLOW
RATTLE

VIVIPAROUS
FESCUE

YELLOW
OXYTROPIS

BOG
WHORTLE-
-BERRY

ROCK
WHITLOW
GRASS

DWARF
CUDWEED

STARWORT
MOUSE-
-EAR
CHICKWEED

MOUNTAIN
PANSY

Black sedge
Carex atrata

Mud Sedge
Carex limosa

Alpine Lettuce
Mulgedium alpinum

Yellow Oxytropis
Oxytropis campestris

Yellow Rattle
Rhinanthus minor

**(Silver) Lady's
Mantle**
Alchemilla conjuncta

Viviparous Fescue
Festuca vivipara

Rock Whitlow Grass
Draba norvegica

Dwarf Cudweed
*Gnaphalium
supinum*

Bog Whortle-berry
*Vaccinium
uliginosum*

**Starwort Mouse-ear
Chickweed**
*Cerastium
cerastoides*

Mountain Pansy
Viola lutea

Margaret's notes:

Alpine Lettuce: v. rare,
rock ledges out of
deer reach

Yellow Oxytropis: v.
rare, rock & scree
(Glen Clova)

Mountain Pansy:
usually yellow but
purple on Ben Lawers

Black Sedge:
(Ben Lawers and
Helvellyn)

Lady's Mantle:
(Glen Doll)

Great Spearwort
Ranunculus lingua

Codlins & Cream
Epilobium hirsutum

Water Violet
Hottonia palustris

Brandybottle
Nuphar lutea

Celery-leaved Crowfoot
Ranunculus sceleratus

Arrowhead
Sagittaria latifolia

Floating Polygonum
Persicaria amphibia

Frogbit
Hydrocharis morsus-ranae

Margaret's notes:

Location: Bruton (Sedgemoor); except Great Spearwort from Newick (also Esthwaite Fen & New Forest)

Brandybottle = Yellow Waterlily

Codlins & Cream - Greater Willowherb

JULY

CODLINS AND CREAM

GREAT SPEAR WORT

WATER VIOLET

BRANDY BOTTLE

CELERY LEAVED CROWFOOT

ARROW HEAD

FLOATING POLYGONUM

FROG BIT

Flowering Rush
Butomus umbellatus

Yellow Loosestrife
Lysimachia vulgaris

Bulrush
Scirpus lacustris

Purple Loosestrife
Lythrum salicaria

Great Water Plantain
Alisma plantago-aquatica

Bur Marigold
Bidens sp.

Sweet Sedge
Acorus calamus

(Greater) Skullcap
Scutellaria laterifolia

JULY

FLOWERING RUSH

YELLOW LOOSESTRIFE

BULRUSH

PURPLE LOOSESTRIFE

GREAT WATER PLANTAIN

BUR MARIGOLD

SWEET SEDGE

SKULLCAP

Margaret's notes:

Location: Benson-on-Thames

Skullcap = Greater Skullcap

Water Stitchwort
Stellaria aquaticum

Hedge Sison
Sison amomum

Canary Grass
Phalaris canariensis

Lesser Water Parsnip
Berula erecta

Sticky Musk
Mimulus moschatus

Lancashire Cranesbill
Geranium sanguineum var. lancastriense

(Common) Winter Green
Pyrola minor

Sea Purslane
Halimione portulacoides

Margaret's notes:

Locations: Lancashire sandhills (Freshfield & Walney Island), except Water Stitchwort, Hedge Sison, Sticky Musk (Sussex)

Water Stitchwort = Chickweed

CURLED DOCK

HIMALAYAN BALSAM

BROAD BLYSMUS

JULY

COMMON

SEA LAVENDER

CREEPING RESTHARROW

Curled Dock
Rumex crispus

Himalayan Balsam
Impatiens glandulifera

Broad Blysmus
Blysmus compressus

Common Sea Lavender
Limonium vulgare

Creeping Restharrow
Ononis repens

Margaret's notes:

Location: Cumbria

Curled Dock, Sea Lavender and Blysmus (Eskmeals Nature Reserve)

(Common) Lime
Tilia x europaea

Wood Burdock
Arctium nemorosum

Greater Bird's-foot Trefoil
Lotus pedunculatus

Dwarf Mallow
Malva neglecta

Alsike Clover
Trifolium hybridum

Marjoram
Origanum majorana

Thyme
Thymus vulgaris

Margaret's notes:

Location: Thornton-le-Dale

Dwarf Mallow also drawn for August

LIME

WOOD BUR-DOCK

GREATER BIRDS FOOT TREFOIL

DWARF MALLOW

JULY

ALSIKE CLOVER

MARJORAM

THYME

JULY

Wood Loosestrife
Lysimachia nemorum

Tormentil
Potentilla erecta

(Common) Centaury
Centaurium erythraea

Ivy-leaved Bell-flower
Wahlenbergia hederacea

Trailing St. John's Wort
Hypericum humifusum

Lesser Toadflax
Chaenorhinum minus

Lesser Water-plantain
Baldellia ranunculoides

Marsh Speedwell
Veronica scutellata

(Greater) Sand Spurrey
Spergularia media

Sundew
Drosera rotundifolia

Pale Butterwort
Pinguicula lusitanica

Yellow Cicendia
Cicendia filiformis

Margaret's notes:

Location: Beaulieu, New Forest

Wood Cudweed
Gnaphalium sylvaticum

Whortle Willow
Salix myrsinites

(Alpine or) Black Bearberry (in fruit)
Arctostaphylos alpina

Holly Fern
Cyrtomium falcatum

Variegated Horsetail
Equisetum variegatum

Curved Sedge
Carex maritima

Serrated Wintergreen
Orthilia secunda

Primula scotica
Primula scotica

Three-Flowered Rush
Juncus triglumis

Cloud-berry (in fruit)
Rubus chamaemorus

Creeping Goodyera
Goodyera repens

Dwarf Cornel (in fruit)
Cornus suecica

Hoary Whitlow Grass
Draba incana

Medium Wintergreen
Pyrola media

Purple Mountain Milk Vetch
Astragalis hypoglottis

WOOD CUDWEED

WHORTLE WILLOW

BLACK BEARBERRY (IN FRUIT)

HOLLY FERN

VARIEGATED HORSE TAIL

CURVED SEDGE

SERRATED WINTER-GREEN

PRIMULA SCOTICA

THREE FLOWERED RUSH

CLOUD-BERRY (IN FRUIT)

JULY

DWARF CORNEL (IN FRUIT)

CREEPING GOODYERA

HOARY WHITLOW GRASS

PURPLE MOUNTAIN MILK VETCH

MEDIUM WINTER-GREEN

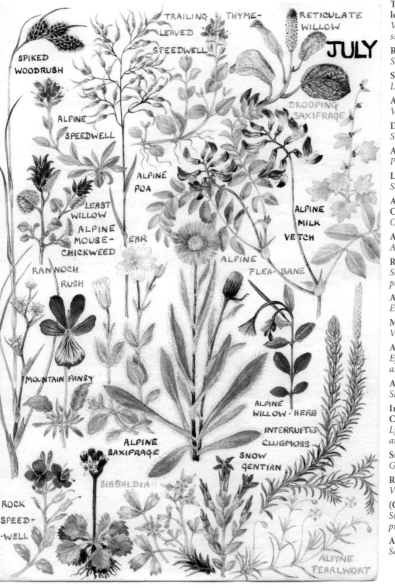

Trailing Thyme-leaved Speedwell
Veronica serpyllifolia ssp. humifusa

Reticulate Willow
Salix reticulata

Spiked Woodrush
Luzula spicata

Alpine Speedwell
Veronica alpina

Drooping Saxifrage
Saxifraga cernua

Alpine Poa
Poa alpina

Least Willow
Salix herbacea

Alpine Mouse-ear Chickweed
Cerastium alpinum

Alpine Milk-vetch
Astragalus alpinus

Rannoch Rush
Scheuchzeria palustris

Alpine Flea-bane
Erigeron borealis

Mountain Pansy
Viola lutea

Alpine Willowherb
Epilobium anaglallidifolium

Alpine Saxifrage
Saxifraga nivalis

Interrupted Clubmoss
Lycopodium annotinum

Snow Gentian
Gentiana nivalis

Rock Speedwell
Veronica fruticans

(Creeping) Sibbaldia
Sibbaldia procumbens

Alpine Pearlwort
Sagina saginoides

Sticky Bartsia
Parentucellia viscosa

Marsh Helleborine
Epipactis palustris

Sea Pea
Lathyrus japonicus

Yellow-wort
Blackstonia perfoliata

Dorset Heath
Erica ciliaris

Sea Bindweed
Calystegia soldanella

English Sundew
Drosera anglica

Margaret's notes:

Location: Dorset (Arne & Chesil Beach etc.)

English Sundew = Great Sundew: common in Scotland

JULY

STICKY BARTSIA

MARSH HELLEBORINE

SEA PEA

YELLOW WORT

DORSET HEATH

SEA BINDWEED

ENGLISH SUNDEW

104

WOOLLY THISTLE

SUCCORY

OX
TONGUE

DROOPING
THISTLE

PYRAMIDAL
ORCHIS

PALE
TOAD-
FLAX

CATHARTIC
FLAX

JULY

SQUINANCYWORT

WHITE
BRYONY

Woolly Thistle
Cirsium eriophorum

Succory
Cichorium intybus

Ox Tongue
Picris echioides

Drooping Thistle
Carduus nutans

Pyramidal Orchis
Anacamptis pyramidalis

Pale Toadflax
Linaria repens

Cathartic Flax
Linum catharticum

Squinancywort
Asperula cynanchica

White Bryony (berries)
Bryonia alba

Margaret's notes:

Location: Benson (Oxford)

Succory = Chicory

Cathartic Flax = Fairy Flax

White Bryony flowers - June

105

Dark Helleborine*
Epipactis atrorubens

Giant Bellflower
Campanula latifolia

Marsh Cinquefoil
Potentilla palustris

Shore Weed
Littorella uniflora

Alpine Lady's Mantle
Alchemilla alpina

Fir Clubmoss
Lycopodium selago

Water Lobelia
Lobelia dortmanna

Margaret's notes:

Location: Kendal (Lakes & Arnside)

*more commonly called Dark Red Helleborine

106

Flote-grass
Glyceria fluitans

Marsh bedstraw
Galium palustre

Reed Grass
Phalaris arundinacea

Common Spike-rush
Eleocharis palustris

Whorled Caraway
Carum verticillatum

Snapdragon
Antirrhinum majus

Climbing Fumitory
Fumaria muralis ssp boraei

Margaret's notes:

Flote Grass: semi-floating, wet places

Reed-grass: riverbanks, wet places

Common Spike-rush: riverbanks, wet places

Whorled Caraway (Galloway) grassy places

Snapdragon: ruins, castle walls

FLOTE-GRASS

MARSH BEDSTRAW

JULY

REED GRASS

COMMON SPIKE-RUSH

WHORLED CARAWAY

SNAPDRAGON

CLIMBING FUMITORY

Spear Plume Thistle
Cirsium vulgare

Cotton Thistle
Onopordum acanthium

Greater Hemp Nettle*
Galeopsis speciosa

Pale Persicaria
Persicaria lapathifolia

Margaret's notes:

Location: Kendal, except Spear Plume Thistle (Sussex)

*also known as the Large-flowered Hemp Nettle

SPEAR PLUME THISTLE

COTTON THISTLE

GREATER HEMP NETTLE

JULY

PALE PERSICARIA

WOAD

BLOOD-DROP

EMLETS

JULY

WATER
SOLDIER

REATER

LADDER WORT

WHORLED WATER-MILFOIL

Woad
Isatis tinctoria

Blood-drop Emlets
Mimulus luteus

Water Soldier
Stratiotes aloides

Greater Bladderwort*
Utricularia vulgaris

Whorled Water-milfoil
Myriophyllum verticillatum

Margaret's notes:

Locations: Woad (Chiswick Palladian Villa); Blood-drop Emlets (Isle of Lewis); Greater Bladderwort (Westmorland); Water Soldier and Whorled Water-milfoil (Strumpshaw Fen, Norfolk)

*also appears on page 82 as Common Bladderwort

109

Broad-leaved Willowherb
Epilobium montanum

Sticky Musk
Mimulus moschatus

Wall Lettuce
Lactuca muralis

Good King Henry
Chenopodium bonus-henricus

Figwort
Scrophularia nodosa

Dewberry
Rubus trivialis

JULY

BROAD
LEAVED
WILLOW- HERB
STICKY
MUSK
WALL
LETTUCE
GOOD
KING
HENRY
FIG-
WORT
DEW-
BERRY

Margaret's notes:

Location: Kendal; except Sticky Musk (Sussex)

110

JULY

MEADOW SWEET

OPIUM POPPY

HEDGE MUSTARD

AUTUMNAL HAWKBIT

Meadowsweet
Filipendula ulmaria

Opium Poppy
Papaver somniferum

Hedge Mustard
Sisymbrium officinale

Autumnal Hawkbit
Scorzoneroides autumnalis

Margaret's notes:

The true Opium Poppy, uncommon now, is white.

111

Bird Cherry (fruit)
Prunus padus

Pendulous Helleborine
Epipactis phyllanthes

Long-headed Poppy
Papaver dubium

Common Sowthistle
Sonchus oleraceus

Crow Garlic
Allium vineale

Storksbill
Erodium cicutarium

Hop (F & M)
Humulus lupulus

Acaena (Pirri-pirri Bur)
Acaenia novae-zelandiae

Margaret's notes:

Acaenia = Pirri-pirri Bur (introduced on Holy Island)

Pendulous helleborine: uncommon, duneslacks (Lancs)

Bird Cherry (N. England) flowers - May

Common Sowthistle: leaves very variable

JULY-AUGUST

DON'S TWITCH

SMOOTH HAWKS-BEARD

CORN SPURREY

TWIN-FLOWER, LINNAEA

COMMON BURNET SAXIFRAGE

ALPINE SAW-WORT

LESSER SWINE-CRESS

Common Burnet Saxifrage
Pimpinella saxifraga

Don's Twitch
Agropyron donianum

Alpine Saw-wort
Saussurea alpina

Smooth Hawk's-beard
Crepis capillaries

Corn Spurrey
Spergula arvensis

Twin-flower (Linnaea)
Linnaea borealis

Lesser Swine-cress
Coronopus didymus

Margaret's notes:

Locations;
Don's Twitch (Inchnadamph);
Linnaea (Scotland), rare; Alpine Saw-wort (Helvellyn)

113

Hemlock
*Conium
maculatum*

Hogweed
*Heracleum
mantegazzianum*

Lovage
*Levisticum
officinale*

**Knotted Hedge
Parsley**
Torilis nodosa

HEMLOCK

HOGWEED

LOVAGE

KNOTTED
HEDGE
PARSLEY

AUGUST

Margaret's notes:

Lovage (Holy
Island): indicated
by red arrows

Hogweed indicated
by green arrows

AUGUST
PLOUGHMAN'S SPIKENARD

CREEPING THISTLE

NARROW-LEAVED RAGWORT

JAPANESE BUCKWHEAT

WATER MINT

Ploughman's Spikenard
Inula conyza

Creeping Thistle
Cirsium arvense

Narrow-leaved Ragwort
Senecio inaequidens

Water Mint
Mentha aquatica

Japanese Buckwheat
Fagopyrum esculentum

Margaret's notes:

Narrow-leaved Ragwort (Southern England)

Japanese Buckwheat: introduced, up to 5 feet high

Ploughman's Spikenard: chalk & limestone

Sweet Chestnut
Castanea sativa

Hemp Agrimony
Eupatorium cannabinum

Upright Hedge Parsley
Torilis japonica

Carline Thistle
Carlina vulgaris

Stink-weed*
Thlaspi arvense

Clustered Bellflower (Campanula)
Campanula glomerata

AUGUST

SWEET CHESTNUT

HEMP AGRIMONY

UP- RIGHT HEDGE PARSLEY

CARLINE THISTLE

STINK- WEED

CLUSTERED BELL -FLOWER (CAMPAN- -ULA)

Margaret's notes:
Location: Sussex

*also appears as Penny Cress on page 17

116

Hawkweed
Hieracium lachenalii

Knot Grass
Polygonum aviculare

Dyer's Rocket*
Reseda luteola

Fennel
Foeniculum vulgare

Annual Mercury
Mercurialis annua

Margaret's notes:

Location: South coast mostly

*also appears on page 64 as Wild Mignonette

Galinsoga
Galinsoga parviflora

Red Alpine Currant*
Ribes alpinum

Black Nightshade
Solanum nigrum

Corn Sowthistle
Sonchus arvensis

Margaret's notes:

Alpine Red Currant (Dovedale) flowers - March

Galinsoga parviflora (Leatherhead Firestation)

Black Nightshade (Northants)

Corn Sowthistle: anywhere

*also appears as Mountain Currant on page 8

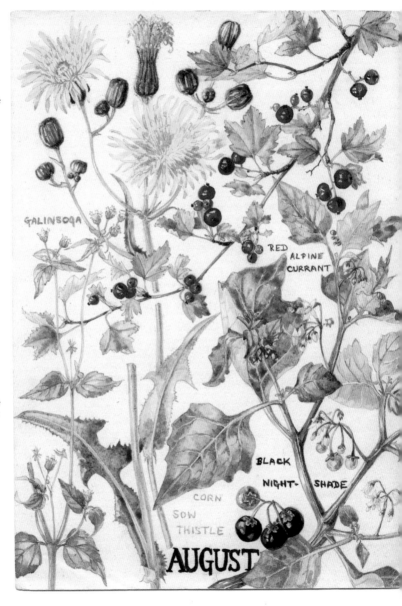

GALINSOGA

RED ALPINE CURRANT

BLACK NIGHT- SHADE

CORN SOW THISTLE

AUGUST

AUGUST

Small Teazel
Dipsacus pilosus

Pennyroyal
Mentha pulegium

Marsh Woundwort
Stachys palustris

Sea Buckthorn
Hippophae rhamnoides

Broad-leaved Ragwort
Senecio fluviatilis

Hedge Basil
Calamintha Clinopodium

Dwarf Mallow
Malva neglecta

Ludwigia*
Ludwigia palustris

Illecebrum**
Illecebrum verticillatum

Pellitory on the Wall
Parietaria officinalis

Margaret's notes:

Location: mostly New Forest; except Broadleaved Ragwort from Bruton

*English name: Hampshire-purslane
**English name: Coral-necklace

Labels on illustration: SMALL TEAZEL, PENNYROYAL, MARSH WOUNDWORT, SEA BUCK-THORN, BROAD-LEAVED RAGWORT, HEDGE BASIL, DWARF MALLOW, LUDWIGIA, ILLECEBRUM, PELLITORY ON THE WALL

119

White Mignonette
Reseda alba

Small Bugloss
Anchusa arvensis

Golden Samphire
Limbarda crithmoides

Sea Kale
Crambe maritima

Rock Sea Lavender
Limonium binervosum

Margaret's notes:
Location: Rhossili & Gower

120

Ash keys
Fraxinus excelsior

Rowan (berries)
Sorbus aucuparia

Wood Groundsel
Senecio sylvaticus

Snow-berry (in fruit)
Symphoricarpos albus

Chickweed Willowherb
Epilobium alsinifolium

Grass of Parnassus
Parnassia palustris

Yellow Corydalis
Pseudofumaria lutea

Crowberry (in fruit)
Empetrum nigrum

Margaret's notes:

Location: Sussex; except Crowberry, Chickweed Willow-herb & Grass of Parnassus (Lake District) and Yellow Corydalis (Thornton-le-Dale)

Ash flowers - April
Rowan flowers - May

121

Cat's-ear
Hypochoeris radicata

Yarrow
Achillea millefolium

Soapwort
Saponaria officinalis

Sea Aster
Aster tripolium

Black Bindweed
Fallopia convolvulus

Sea Holly
Eryngium maritimum

Margaret's notes:

Location: Bamburgh & Warkworth

122

AUGUST

MARSH
SOWTHISTLE

Marsh Sowthistle
Sonchus palustris

Wild Radish
Raphanus raphanistrum

Parsley
Petroselinum crispum

WILD
RADISH

PARSLEY

Margaret's notes:

Locations: Wild Radish (Suffolk coast); Marsh Sowthistle (Strumpshaw Fen, Burndale); 7' tall Parsley (Cadgwith, Cornwall)

Water Pepper
Persicaria hydropiper

Hair-leaved Goldilocks
Linosyris vulgaris

Black Horehound
Ballota nigra

Scentless Mayweed
Matricaria inodora

Cudweed
Filago vulgaris

Dune Helleborine
Epipactis dunensis

Common Bartsia
Odontites verna

Juniper
Juniperus communis

Margaret's notes:

Hair-leaved Goldilocks (Humphrey Head)

Dune Helleborine (Sandscale, Barrow)

Epipactis leptochila var. dunensis* (Sandscale Haws)

Black Horehound (Suffolk); Scentless Mayweed has no scales between disk florets; Chamomiles (Chamomilla or anthemis) have scales [see June]

*now Epipactis dunensis

AUGUST

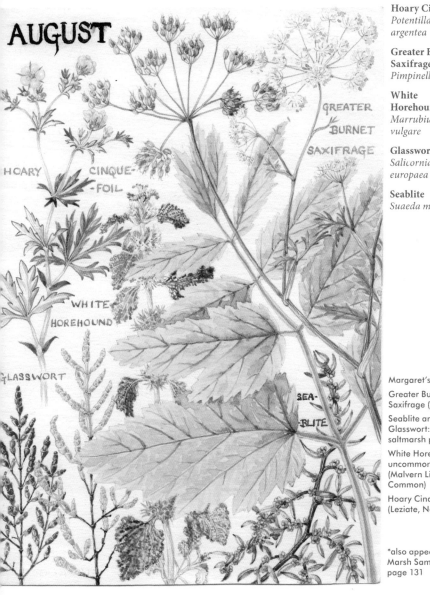

HOARY CINQUE-
-FOIL

GREATER
BURNET
SAXIFRAGE

WHITE
HOREHOUND

GLASSWORT

SEA-
-BLITE

Hoary Cinquefoil
Potentilla argentea

Greater Burnet Saxifrage
Pimpinella major

White Horehound
Marrubium vulgare

Glasswort*
Salicornia europaea

Seablite
Suaeda maritima

Margaret's notes:

Greater Burnet Saxifrage (Ripon)

Seablite and Glasswort: saltmarsh plants

White Horehound, uncommon (Malvern Link Common)

Hoary Cinquefoil (Leziate, Norfolk)

*also appears as Marsh Samphire on page 131

Marsh Mallow
Althaea officinalis

Elecampane
Inula helenium

Corn Woundwort
Stachys arvensis

Sea Spleenwort
*Asplenium
marinum*

Sea Heath
Frankenia laevis

Borage
Borago officinalis

**Knotted
Pearlwort**
Sagina nodosa

MARSH
MALLOW

ELECAMPANE

AUGUST

CORN
WOUND-
WORT

SEA
SPLEENWORT

SEA
HEATH

BORAGE

KNOTTED
PEARLWORT

Margaret's notes:

St. David's (except
Marsh Mallow and
Sea Heath from
Rye)

AUGUST

COWBANE

ANGELICA

COMMON
STINGING
NETTLE

SWEET
CICELY
(FRUIT)

Cowbane
Cicuta virosa

Angelica
*Angelica
archangelica*

**Common
Stinging Nettle**
Urtica dioica

**Sweet Cicely
(fruit)**
Myrrhis odorata

Margaret's notes:

Cowbane
(Strumpshaw
Reserve, Norfolk)

White Melilot
Melilotus albus

Sticky Groundsel
Senecio viscosus

Agrimony
Agrimonia eupatoria

Sea Radish
Raphanus maritimus

Cornish Heath
Erica vagans

Burnet Rose (hips)
Rosa spinosissima

Rupture-wort
Herniaria glabra

Small-flowered Catchfly
Silene gallica

Lesser Snapdragon
Misopates orontium

Margaret's notes:

Cornwall (Gweek, Lizard)

Burnet Rose flowers in June

WHITE MELILOT

AUGUST

STICKY GROUNDSEL

AGRIMONY

SEA RADISH

CORNISH HEATH

HIPS OF BURNET ROSE

RUPTURE WORT

SMALL-FLOWERED CATCHFLY

LESSER SNAP DRAGON

FOOL'S PARSLEY

AUGUST

RAYLESS
MAYWEED

ROSEBAY

DEADLY
NIGHT-
-SHADE

DURMAST OAK

HIPS OF
DOWNY
ROSE

Fool's Parsley
Aethusa cynapium

Rayless Mayweed
*Matricaria
matricarioides*

Rosebay
*Epilobium
angustifolium*

**Deadly
Nightshade**
Atropa belladonna

Durmast Oak
Quercus petraea

**Downy Rose
(hips)**
Rosa villosa

Margaret's notes:

Location: Kendal

Deadly Nightshade:
chalk & limestone,
flowers - June

Common Oak - see
also page 140

(Northern) Downy
Rose - R. villosa

Petty Spurge
Euphorbia peplus

Sun Spurge
Euphorbia helioscopia

Greater Bindweed
Calystegia silvatica

Enchanter's Nightshade
Circaea lutetiana

Small Nettle
Urtica urens

Procumbent Pearlwort
Sagina procumbens

Tuberous Pink Sorrel
Oxalis articulata

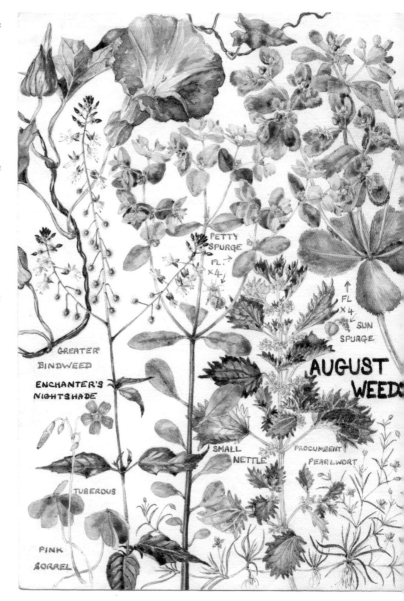

Margaret's notes:
August Weeds

Frosted Orache
Atriplex laciniata

Sea Spurge
Euphorbia paralias

Sea Purslane
Halimione portulacoides

Wild Beet
Beta vulgaris ssp. maritima

Sea Scirpus*
Bolboschoenus maritimus

(Lax-flowered) Sea Lavender
Limonium humile

(Common) Cordgrass
Spartina anglica

(Marsh) Samphire**
Salicornia europaea

Hare's-foot Clover
Trifolium arvense

Strawberry Clover
Trifolium fragiferum

Prickly Saltwort
Kali turgida

Margaret's notes:

Lax-flowered Sea Lavender (Beaulieu)

*Sea Club-rush. The name 'Sea Scirpus' is not generally used but is a 'translation' of Scirpus maritimus, an earlier scientific name.

**also appears as Glasswort on page 125

131

Fuchsia
Fuchsia magellanica

Fern Royal
Osmunda regalis

Arbutus
Arbutus unedo

Rose of Sharon
Hypericum calycinum

Tutsan
Hypericum androsaemum

Margaret's notes:

Arbutus = Strawberry Tree

Location: Ireland; Tutsan (also Sussex & Lake District)

IRISH AUGUST

FUCHSIA

FERN ROYAL

ARBUTUS

ROSE OF SHARON

TUTSAN

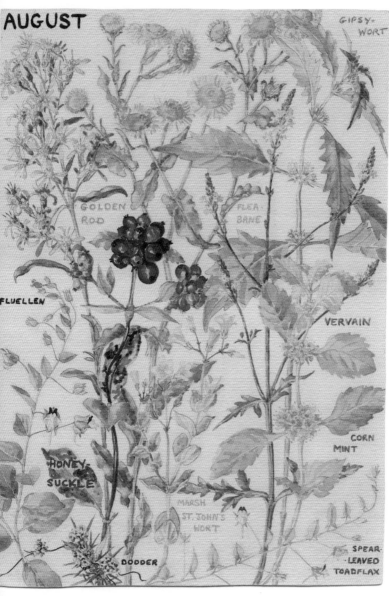

AUGUST

GIPSY-WORT

GOLDEN ROD

FLEA-BANE

FLUELLEN

VERVAIN

HONEY-SUCKLE

MARSH ST. JOHN'S WORT

CORN MINT

SPEAR-LEAVED TOADFLAX

DODDER

Gipsy-wort
Lycopus europaeus

Goldenrod
Solidago virgaurea

Fleabane
Pulicaria dysenterica

Fluellen
Kickxia spuria

Vervain
Verbena officinalis

Corn Mint
Mentha arvensis

Honeysuckle
Lonicera perclymenum

Marsh St. John's Wort
Hypericum elodes

Dodder
Cuscuta epithymum

Spear-leaved Toadflax
Kickxia elatine

Margaret's notes:
Honeysuckle
flowers - May

133

Knapweed
Centaurea nigra

Ragwort
Senecio jacobaea

Convolvulus*
Calystegia sepium

Round-headed Rampion
Phyteuma orbiculare

(Field) Bindweed
Convolvulus arvensis

Margaret's notes:

Location: West Walton; except Round-headed Rampion from Sussex & Wilts: chalk

*what Margaret called Convolvulus is the Hedge Bindweed, which used to be Convolvulus sepium and is now Calystegia sepium. What she called Bindweed is known as Field Bindweed.

AUGUST

KNAP WEED

RAGWORT

CONVOLVULUS

ROUND-HEADED RAMPION

BINDWEED

YELLOW
MELILOT

AUGUST

CORN
PARSLEY

LIVELONG

SAND
DUNE

PANSY

WALL
MUSTARD

KNOTTED

HEDGE

PARSLEY

WORMWOOD

Yellow Melilot
Melilotus officinalis

Corn Parsley
Petroselinum segetum

Livelong
Hylotelephium telephium

Sand-dune Pansy
Viola curtisii

Wall Mustard
Diplotaxis muralis

Knotted Hedge Parsley
Torilis nodosa

Wormwood
Artemisia absinthium

Margaret's notes:

Location: St. David's & Sussex, except Wall Mustard from Bristol

Pearl Antennaria
Antennaria margaritacea

(Marsh) Arrow Grass
Triglochin palustris

Corn Marigold
Chrysanthemum segetum

(Common) Camomile
Anthemis nobilis

Bog Myrtle (Sweet Gale)
Myrica Gale

(Common) Cow-wheat
Melampyrum pratense

Purple Molinia
Molinia caerulea

(Summer) Ladies' Tresses
Spiranthes aestivalis

Water Purslane
Lythrum portula

Tufted Vetch
Vicia cracca

Margaret's notes:

Location: Beaulieu, except Corn Marigold from Benson

Bog Myrtle - flowers April

Marsh Arrow-grass (not Sea) flowers May

AUGUST

PEARL ANTENNARIA

ARROW GRASS

CORN MARIGOLD

CAMOMILE

BOG MYRTLE (SWEET GALE)

COW WHEAT

PURPLE MOLINIA

LADIES' TRESSES

WATER PURSLANE

TUFTED VETCH

136

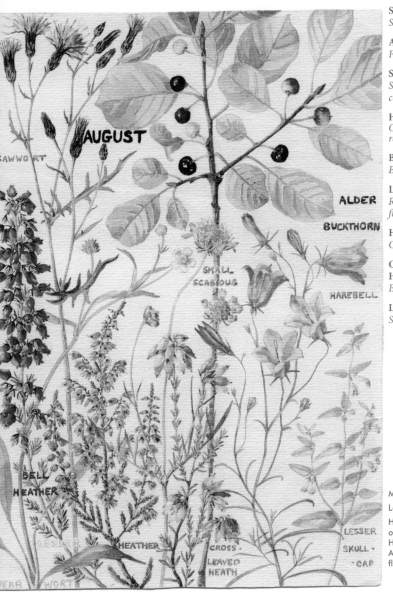

Saw-wort
Serratula tinctoria

Alder Buckthorn
Frangula alnus

Small Scabious
Scabiosa columbaria

Harebell
Campanula rotundifolia

Bell Heather
Erica cinerea

Lesser Spearwort
Ranunculus flammula

Heather (Ling)
Calluna vulgaris

Cross-leaved Heath
Erica tetralix

Lesser Skullcap
Scutellaria minor

AUGUST

SAWWORT

ALDER
BUCKTHORN

SMALL
SCABIOUS

HAREBELL

BELL
HEATHER

LESSER

HEATHER

CROSS-

LEAVED
HEATH

LESSER
SKULL-
-CAP

SPEAR-WORT

Margaret's notes:

Location: Sussex

Harebell = Bluebell of Scotland
Heather = Ling
Alder Buckthorn flowers in May

137

Dwarf Elder or Danewort
Sambucus ebulus

Wild Parsnip
Pastinaca sativa

Fringed water-lily
Nymphoides peltata

Mugwort
Artemisia ludoviciana

DWARF ELDER,

DANE-

-WORT

AUGUST

WILD

PARSNIP

FRINGED
WATER-LILY

MUGWORT

Margaret's notes:

Location: Sussex; except Fringed Water-lily (Furnace pond, Slaugham)

Mugwort = Artemisia

MIDLAND HAWTHORN

DEWBERRY

BANEBERRY

HORNBEAM

DWARF ELDER →

PALE DWARF FURZE

SEPTEMBER

ALPINE ENCHANTER'S NIGHTSHADE

Midland Hawthorn (haws)
Crataegus laevigata

Dewberry (fruits)
Rubus caesius

Baneberry (fruits)
Actaea spicata

Hornbeam (fruits)
Carpinus betulus

Dwarf Elder (fruits)
Sambucus ebulus

Alpine Enchanter's Nightshade
Circaea alpina x lutetiana

Pale Dwarf Furze
Ulex minor

Margaret's notes:

Dwarf Furze (St. David's)

Midland Hawthorn (Sibford, Bambury)

Hornbeam (Sussex)

Dwarf Elder = Danewort (Sussex, S. Downs)

Alpine Enchanter's Nightshade: hybrid (Aira Force, Ullswater)

Baneberry = Herb Christopher (Ingleborough)

Elder (berries)
Sambucus nigra

Hazel Nut
Corylus avellana

Whitebeam
Sorbus aria

Guelder Rose (in fruit)
Viburnum opulus

Wayfaring Tree
Viburnum lantana

Acorn (Pedunculate Oak)
Quercus robur

Margaret's notes:

Location: Bruton

Wayfaring Tree = Mealy Guelder Rose

All flower in May, except Hazel which has catkins in February

SEPTEMBER

ELDER

HAZEL NUT

WHITE BEAM

GUELDER ROSE

WAYFARING TREE

ACORN

Traveller's Joy
Clematis vitalba

Devil's-bit Scabious
Succisa pratensis

Blackberry
Rubus fruticosus

Old Man's Beard
Clematis recta

Autumn Crocus
Colchicum autumnale

Lords & Ladies
Arum maculatum

Marsh Gentian
Gentiana pneumonanthe

Calamint
Calamintha ascendens

SEPTEMBER

TRAVELLER'S JOY

DEVIL'S -BIT SCABIOUS

BLACK-BERRY

OLD MAN'S BEARD

AUTUMN CROCUS LORDS & LADIES

MARSH GENTIAN

CALAMINT

Margaret's notes:

Location: Bruton; except Marsh Gentian (Ashdown Forest)

Autumn Crocus = Meadow Saffron

Autumn Crocus fruits in May

Sycamore fruit
Acer pseudoplatanus

Broom cods
Cytisus scoparius

Touch-me-not (Yellow Balsam)
Impatiens noli-tangere

Small balsam
Impatiens parviflora

Common Hemp-nettle
Galeopsis tetrahit

North American Loosestrife
Lysimachia terrestris

Cranberry (in fruit)
Oxycoccus palustris

Margaret's notes:

Yellow Balsam (Windermere & Coniston Water)

N. American Loosestrife (Windermere: naturalised)

Broom and Sycamore flower in May

Cranberry: on sphagnum bog, flowers - June

SEPTEMBER

YEW

HORSE CHESTNUT

HOPS

IRIS

BUCKTHORN

Yew
Taxus baccata

Horse Chestnut (Conkers)
Aesculus hippocastanus

Hops
Humulus lupulus

(Stinking) Iris (in fruit)
Iris foetidissima

Buckthorn (in fruit)
Rhamnus cathartica

Margaret's notes:

Location: Bruton

Yew - flowers March

Horse Chestnut = Conkers, flowers in May

Buckthorn - flowers May

Stinking Iris - flowers June

Black Bryony (in fruit)
Tamus communis

Haws (Hawthorn)
Crataegus monogyna

Hips (Dog Rose)
Rosa canina

(Field) Maple (keys)
Acer campestre

Sloe (Blackthorn)
Prunus spinosa

Dogwood (in fruit)
Cornus sanguinea

Margaret's notes:

Location: Bruton

Sloe = Blackthorn - flowers April

Maple - flowers May*

Dog Rose, Wild Rose: flowers June

Hawthorn = May, flowers in May

Dogwood, flowers June

*Margaret's painting of Maple in flower is shown on page 14, for April, not May

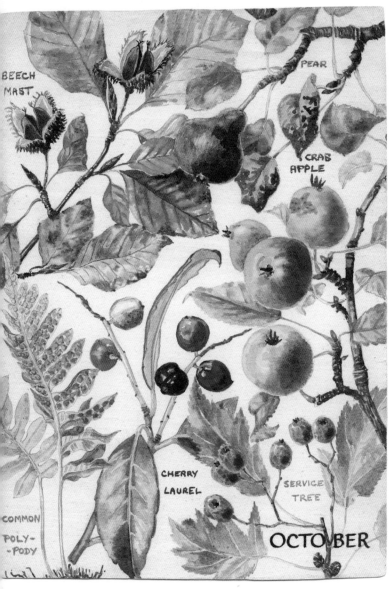

Beech mast
Fagus sylvatica

Pear (in fruit)
Pyrus communis

Crab Apple (in fruit)
Malus sylvestris

Common Polypody
Polypodium vulgare

Cherry Laurel (in fruit)
Prunus laurocerasus

(Wild) Service Tree (in fruit)
Sorbus torminalis

Margaret's notes:

Location: Sussex; except Polypody (Bruton)

Pear*, Crab Apple, Cherry Laurel - all flower in May

*Margaret's painting of Pear in flower is shown on page 12, for April, not May

BEECH MAST

PEAR

CRAB APPLE

CHERRY LAUREL

SERVICE TREE

COMMON POLY-PODY

OCTOBER

145

**Privet
(in fruit)**
Ligustrum vulgare

Spindle (in fruit)
*Euonymus
europaeus*

Ivy (in fruit)
Hedera helix

**Rusty-back
(Fern)**
*Asplenium
ceterach*

NOVEMBER

PRIVET

SPINDLE

IVY

RUSTY
BACK

Margaret's notes:

Location: Bruton

Privet flowers - June

Spindle flowers -
June

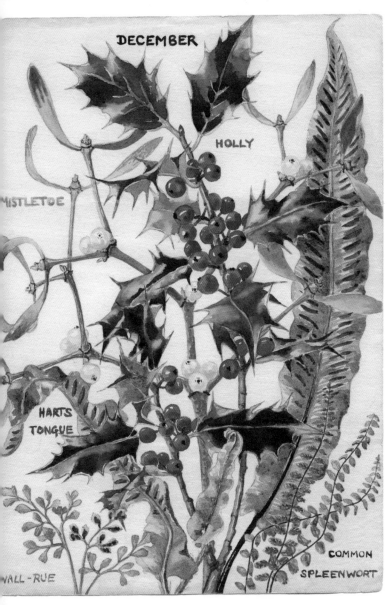

DECEMBER

HOLLY

MISTLETOE

HARTS
TONGUE

WALL-RUE

COMMON
SPLEENWORT

Holly (in fruit)
Ilex aquifolium

Mistletoe (in fruit)
Viscum album

Hart's Tongue
Asplenium scolopendrium

Wall-rue
Asplenium ruta-muraria

Common Spleenwort
Asplenium trichomanes

Margaret's notes:
Location: Bruton
Holly flowers - May

147

Common Lungwort

Index of Common Names

Index of Scientific Names

Index of Scientific Names

Also published by Merlin Unwin Books (more details: www.merlinunwin.co.uk)

Woodland Wild Flowers *through the seasons*

My Wood

Wildlife of the Pennine Hills

Hedgerow Medicine *harvest and make your own herbal remedies*

Wayside Medicine *forgotten plants and how to use them*

A Kaleidoscope of Butterflies *a celebration of Britain's 59 species*

A Murmuration of Starlings *the collective nouns of animals and birds*

A String of Pearls *the landscape and literature of the Lake District*